# DK POCKET EYEWITNESS

# INVENTIONS

## FACTS AT YOUR FINGERTIPS

 Penguin
Random
House

**DK DELHI**
**Senior editor** Bharti Bedi
**Project art editor** Isha Nagar
**Jacket designer** Priyanka Bansal
**Jackets editorial coordinator** Priyanka Sharma
**DTP designers** Jaypal Singh Chauhan, Ashok Kumar
**Picture researcher** Sakshi Saluja
**Managing jackets editor** Saloni Talwar
**Managing editor** Kingshuk Ghoshal
**Managing art editor** Govind Mittal
**Pre-production manager** Balwant Singh
**Production manager** Pankaj Sharma

**DK LONDON**
**Senior editor** Caroline Stamps
**Senior art editor** Rachael Grady
**Managing editor** Linda Esposito
**Managing art editor** Philip Letsu
**Jacket designer** Surabhi Wadhwa-Gandhi
**Jacket editor** Emma Dawson
**Jacket design development manager** Sophia MTT
**Producer (pre-production)** Jacqueline Street
**Producer (print production)** Vivienne Yong

**Publisher** Andrew Macintyre
**Associate publishing director** Liz Wheeler
**Art director** Karen Self
**Design director** Phil Ormerod
**Publishing director** Jonathan Metcalf

**Consultant** Roger Bridgman

This edition published in 2019
First published in Great Britain in 2016
by Dorling Kindersley Limited
80 Strand, London WC2R 0RL

Copyright © 2016, 2019 Dorling Kindersley Limited
A Penguin Random House Company
10 9 8 7 6 5 4 3 2 1
001–310509–May/19

A CIP catalogue record for this book
is available from the British Library.

ISBN: 978-0-2413-4358-6

Printed and bound in China

A WORLD OF IDEAS:
**SEE ALL THERE IS TO KNOW**

**www.dk.com**

# CONTENTS

### Scales and sizes
This book contains scale drawings of most of the inventions mentioned to indicate their size.

3.3 m (11 ft)    1.8 m (6 ft)    15 cm (6 in)    4 cm (1½ in)

**Digital camera**

# What is an invention?

An invention is something that is developed by a person, or by a team of people, usually in response to a need. From paper cups to pencils, good inventions make our lives easier. Other inventions, such as chocolate bars, make our lives more fun.

**Light bulbs** enable work and study into the evening

Lodestone is magnetic

This paperclip "sticks" to it

## What is a discovery?

Discoveries and inventions often complement each other, but they are different things. A discovery is when something that already exists is found. The discovery of lodestone, a naturally magnetic rock, led to the invention of the first compass, used by sailors to navigate.

## Who was first?

Many inventions have been developed by different people at the same time. A famous example is the light bulb, first made by Englishman Joseph Swan and by American Thomas Edison in 1878. The two had not worked together.

## What is a patent?

A patent is a legal document that grants sole rights to an individual or company to make, use, and sell an invention for a certain period of time. A patent protects an original idea, so the inventor can make money from it.

This tin opener was made in 1865

## That's a good idea!

Some inventions meet an obvious need. The first tin opener, invented in 1855, was made almost 60 years after the invention of the sealed tin can; before this, cans were opened with a hammer and chisel.

## INNOVATION

Innovation is the application of better solutions that meet new requirements or needs. For example, the innovations to the light bulb – from incandescent to compact fluorescent to LED – has meant brighter lighting.

Incandescent bulb

Compact fluorescent bulb

LED bulb

# How do they happen?

Not all inventions come about as a result of endless experimentation in a laboratory or workshop (although that is certainly how some have been created). Where other people might throw away their mistakes, inventors are often geniuses who have carried on developing, researching, experimenting, and marketing their ideas.

### If at first you don't succeed...

Sir James Dyson wanted to build a better vacuum cleaner, and he is now well known as the inventor of the bagless vacuum cleaner. However, he had more than 5,100 failures before getting it right. In fact he set up his own manufacturing company as no manufacturer would make his invention.

Bagless vacuum cleaner

James Dyson

### Observation

Mary Anderson noticed drivers wiping their car windows by hand and, in 1903, devised the first windscreen wiper.

## Refinement

Many inventions are refinements of earlier ones. For example, the MP3 player may not have existed if people hadn't invented earlier versions of recording music, or developed (and then miniaturized) computers.

## Curiosity

Kenneth Shinozuka invented a wearable sensor at the age of 15 to alert carers if a patient suffering from Alzheimer's started wandering. He developed it because he was worried about his grandfather.

## ACCIDENTAL INVENTIONS

Some of today's most widely known inventions occurred by chance.

**Cornflakes** were invented by the Kellogg brothers in 1894 from overcooked wheat that they rolled into flakes.

**Matches** were invented by John Walker in 1826 when he discovered that certain chemicals sparked when scraped.

**Microwave ovens** were invented when Percy Spencer found that radar waves had melted some chocolate in his pocket.

# Non-material inventions

Not all inventions are items we can touch, but these "invisible" inventions are just as important in terms of human history. Where would we be if language or counting systems or sports hadn't been invented?

### Government

Government and laws developed with the first civilizations and the need to have rules for large numbers of people living together. This ancient black pillar (only the top is shown here) listed the laws of Babylon, carved in stone. The pillar dates from 1760 BCE.

King receiving laws from **God of Justice**

### Writing

The earliest writing consisted of symbols marked on clay and it was in use for a long time. This clay tablet (dating to around 2350 BCE) was engraved with a count of goats and sheep. Written language (as opposed to symbols) began to emerge in Mesopotamia (modern-day Iraq) in 3200 BCE and in Mesoamerica (modern-day Central America) in 600 BCE.

**Sumerian clay tablet**

## Sports

Many sports have been invented on the back of material inventions. The invention of the ball, for example, has led to all sorts of games – from football to tennis. This stone ring was used for ball games in Mayan communities more than 1,000 years ago.

## Zero

The understanding of zero appeared in India around the fifth century CE. This was a huge leap forward as it allowed people to solve numerical problems to which the answer was "nothing". One of the first people to understand the importance of zero is thought to have been an Indian mathematician called Aryabhata.

**Statue of Aryabhata**

## Number systems

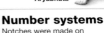

Notches were made on bone, wood, and stone some 40,000 years ago to aid counting. The Ishango bone (left), believed to show columns of numbers represented by notches, dates back 20,000 years.

depictions of animals

# Inventions that failed

For every invention that we see or use every day, there are many thousands that haven't succeeded. Some might work but are just too expensive to take further for a wider market, while others are impractical.

## A truck with legs

Many inventors have tried to develop robots that look like animals, and developments in this area are progressing fast. However, this four-legged beast was heavy and unwieldy to operate. Its inventor, Ralph Mosher, is at the controls in this 1968 photograph.

## Monowheel vehicles

A monowheel vehicle consists of a single wheel, with the driver and engine (if powered) positioned inside it. It was once hoped they would be widely used, but road-safe monowheels are rare.

### Before its time

Even famous inventors fail. Thomas Edison, one of the most famous of all inventors, held 1,093 patents. Not all enjoyed success. For example, he invented a talking doll in 1889. We have talking dolls today, but Edison's was way ahead of the available technology.

### Wooden swimming suits

This picture was taken in 1930 by a timber company to promote wood veneer bathing suits. The suits were marketed as a practical alternative to fabric costumes; they were said to help a swimmer stay afloat!

**Kerry McLean** is one of the few people to have successfully built a number of monowheels

# A brief look at time

There have been a number of significant ages in human history, from the Stone Age to the Information Age. These ages are very much defined by developments in the type of inventions that have emerged and a quickening in the pace of their discovery.

### Stone Age

A huge number of inventions emerged in the Stone Age, from simple tools such as the hand axe to more complicated weapons like the bow and arrow, and from clothing to developments in agricultural tools. Stone Age peoples had to invent to survive, and in the process they created many things still in use today.

**Stone tools** were used by early humans

## Bronze Age

Bronze is an alloy (a mixture) of copper and tin. It was the first metal to be widely used, as it was stronger than copper alone and it could be cast and also hammered into shape.

Molten bronze can be cast in a mould.

## Iron Age

Iron was first used in about 2000 BCE. Its use spread slowly, but it resulted in key developments in different industries. The plough, for example, had already been invented, but the invention of iron tips made it a better tool.

**Modern Sudanese iron knife**

## Industrial Revolution

The mid-1700s saw the beginnings of the Industrial Revolution, a huge period of change that started in Great Britain and would affect industry throughout the world. This was when factories began to appear.

## Information age

We are currently living in an information age. Huge advances are being made in computer technology. This age is also sometimes called the Computer, or Digital Age.

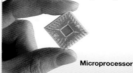

**Microprocessor**

# Transport

We depend on different methods of transport to travel to school and work, to visit friends and to go on holiday. We also depend on efficient transport for all sorts of goods and services. Food produce, for example, is moved around the world by ship and aeroplane, and, more locally, along extensive road networks. Take a look at inventions in the world of transport.

**TRANSPORTING PEOPLE**
It has been estimated that at any one time, around half a million people are in the air, carried in large passenger planes. The first aeroplane only took off in 1903.

# Major transport inventions

Inventions in the area of transport really took off in the 1800s with the invention of the internal combustion engine. There was, however, a particularly important event thousands of years before this: the invention of the wheel.

### Wheel

The wheel (at first in use as a potter's wheel) made it easier to move objects from place to place, which opened up trade.

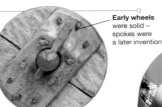

**Early wheels** were solid – spokes were a later invention

### Steam engine

The use of boiling water to create steam that could be used to move objects was recognized by the ancient Greeks. However, the first practical steam engine didn't appear until 1712 with Thomas Newcomen's beam engine.

**Model of early steam locomotive, built by Richard Trevithick c.1808**

# Car engine

Today, most cars have an internal combustion engine in which the fuel is burned inside pistons in the engine, rather than in a boiler (as with a steam engine). The first successful internal combustion engine was built by Jean Joseph Étienne Lenoir in 1860.

**Modern stunt jet fighter**

## Jet engine

A patent for the first jet engine was taken out by a British pilot, Frank Whittle, in 1930 but nobody thought it would work and he failed to find a manufacturer. The first jet-engined plane took off in 1939 in Germany designed by Hans von Ohain.

## Four-stroke engine

As its name suggests, the four-stroke engine uses four strokes of a piston to produce power. Nikolaus Otto's 1876 internal combustion engine is acknowledged as the first four-stroke engine.

Each piston is contained in a cylinder and runs through the same four-stroke cycle dozens of times a second.

**Bugatti Veyron Grand Sport**

**Sports cars** have particularly powerful engines

1. Intake   2. Compression   3. Combustion   4. Exhaust

# Water transport

The first boats were simple, built with readily available materials; it's known that some were made of animal skins stretched over a wooden frame. Such boats would have been limited to lakes and rivers. As technology improved, boats got larger.

FOCUS ON...
**SHIP ANATOMY**
Like cars, boats have special names for their parts.

## Log boat

Prehistoric peoples did use boats. Tree trunks were hollowed out to make simple boats – or rather, heavy canoes. The earliest log boat that has been discovered is known as the Pesse canoe, which was found in The Netherlands and dates back about 10,000 years. It's likely that the first log boats were a lot older than this.

| | |
|---|---|
| **INVENTED BY** | Unknown |
| **WHEN** | 10000 BCE |
| **WHERE** | Unknown |

*Dugout canoes are made from a single tree trunk*

## Sails

It's not known exactly when the first sails appeared, but a pottery disc that appears to show a sailing boat, dating to around 5300 BCE, was found in 2002 in present-day Kuwait. The first seaworthy sailing ships were caravals.

*Early sails only worked if the wind was behind them*

**Portuguese caraval**

| | |
|---|---|
| **INVENTED BY** | Unknown |
| **WHEN** | pre 5300 BCE |
| **WHERE** | Unknown |

▲ The hull is the main body of a boat or ship – the bottom and the sides. It has to be watertight.

*Hull*

▲ A keel runs along the base of a boat or ship. It supports the hull and provides stability.

*Keel*

▶ Rudders are used to steer a boat or ship. They were a fairly late invention.

*Rudder*

## Clinker-built boats

Boats built with separate, overlapping planks are known as "clinker-built". The remains of one clinker-built canoe, the Hjortspring boat, are believed to be at least 2,300 years old.

| INVENTED BY | Unknown |
|---|---|
| WHEN | 400–300 BCE |
| WHERE | Scandinavia |

*Viking longships used a clinker construction method*

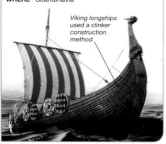

## Submarine

### Replica of Drebbel's submarine

*DREBBEL*

The first submarine was made of wood covered in greased leather. It was very different from the powerful submarines of today; it was propelled by oarsmen and reached a depth of just 4.5 m (12 ft). It is rumoured it once carried the then King of England, James I.

| INVENTED BY | Cornelis Drebbel |
|---|---|
| WHEN | 1620 |
| WHERE | England |

# An amphibious car can travel at up to

# 96 kph (60 mph)

## over water – and even faster on land.

**AMPHIBIOUS VEHICLES**
It took a lot of research and development to produce a car that could easily convert from land use to water use. WaterCar's Panther, shown here, can reach 72 kph (45 mph) on water – a previous car, the Python, could go even faster.

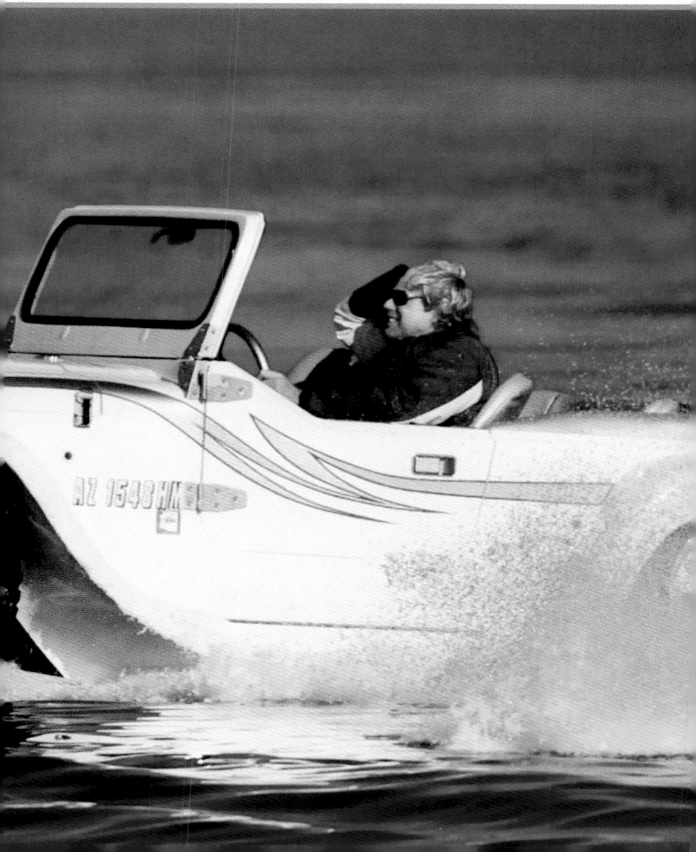
AZ 1548HM

# Land transport

Road networks and rail tracks now cross continents, but there was a time these didn't exist. The development of wheeled vehicles came in response to a growing population and the resulting need to transport heavier goods at a faster pace than before.

### Sledge

Some inventions happen because they are suitable for the immediate surroundings. Wooden sledges emerged around 9,000 years ago in northern Europe, where they were easy to slide over icy ground.

| | |
|---|---|
| **INVENTED BY** | Unknown |
| **WHEN** | c.7000 BCE |
| **WHERE** | Arctic fringes |

**Racing sledge**

### Two-wheeled chariot

The chariot was developed for use by the military as a lightweight alternative to heavy wagons. The first chariots were pulled by animals, such as oxen. Four-wheeled chariots appeared even earlier, dating to between 2600 and 2400 BCE.

| | |
|---|---|
| **INVENTED BY** | Unknown |
| **WHEN** | c.2000 BCE |
| **WHERE** | Mesopotamia (modern-day Iraq) |

*The invention of spoked wheels made the chariot possible*

**Ancient Roman chariot**

## Petrol-powered car

The first petrol-powered car was called a Motorwagen. It had three spoked wheels, a rear engine, and could only reach 13 kph (8 mph). Four-wheeled cars soon followed, from various inventors including Karl Benz and Gottlieb Daimler.

| | |
|---|---|
| **INVENTED BY** | Karl Benz |
| **WHEN** | 1885 |
| **WHERE** | Germany |

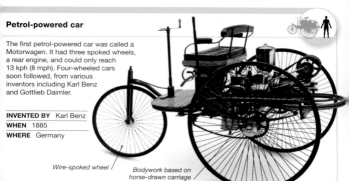

*Wire-spoked wheel*

*Bodywork based on horse-drawn carriage*

## Front engine car

*Steering tiller*

Road cars today have engines at the front, a development that first appeared with Panhard and Levassor's car in the late 1800s. Early cars had a steering tiller rather than a steering wheel.

| | |
|---|---|
| **INVENTED BY** | Rene Panhard and Emile Levassor |
| **WHEN** | 1891 |
| **WHERE** | France |

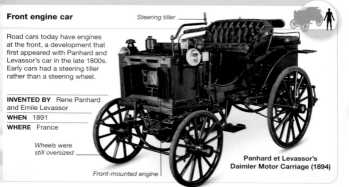

*Wheels were still oversized*

*Front-mounted engine*

**Panhard et Levassor's Daimler Motor Carriage (1894)**

## Dandy horse

The dandy horse was the earliest bicycle. The inventor called it a Laufmaschine (or "running machine"). It had no pedals – the rider simply sat on it and walked or ran. Dandy horses also came to be known as velocipedes.

**INVENTED BY** Baron Karl Drais

**WHEN** 1817

**WHERE** Germany

*A wooden frame made this a heavy bicycle*

## Velocipede

Many bicycles were invented in the 1800s and it can be difficult to pin down the first of each type. This unwieldy wooden machine was the first mass-produced velocipede. It was commonly known as the boneshaker!

**INVENTED BY** Pierre Michaux

**WHEN** 1860s

**WHERE** France

## Penny Farthing

There have been many disagreements as to who can be called the inventor of the Penny Farthing (they are also known as high bicycles). For a long time, James Starley in England was hailed as having built the first. However, Eugène Meyer in France produced a wire-spoked tension-wheeled version a year earlier than Starley.

**INVENTED BY** Eugène Meyer

**WHEN** 1880s

**WHERE** France

*This Penny Farthing race takes place in Cheshire, England, once every 10 years*

The Penny Farthing took its name from two English coins, one (the penny) much larger than the other (the farthing).

## Reitwagen

Although an English inventor, Edward Butler, designed a three-wheeled motorcycle in 1884, the Reitwagen is widely seen as the first motorbike. "Reitwagen" means "riding car".

**INVENTED BY** Gottlieb Daimler and Wilhelm Maybach

**WHEN** 1885

**WHERE** Germany

## Kick scooter

Scooters have been popular for about 100 years. The folding Razor kick scooter was a new type invented in the 1990s. It is made of aluminium, a lightweight metal. The wheels are just 98 mm (3.75 in) in diameter.

**INVENTED BY** Wim Ouboter (micro scooter)

**WHEN** 1998

**WHERE** Switzerland

**Three-wheeled scooter**

## Steam locomotive

Chimney        Boiler

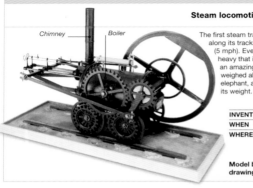

The first steam train chugged along its tracks at the rate of 8 kph (5 mph). Even though it was so heavy that it broke the rails, it was an amazing feat of engineering. It weighed about the same as an adult elephant, and could haul four times its weight.

| | |
|---|---|
| **INVENTED BY** | Richard Trevithick |
| **WHEN** | 1804 |
| **WHERE** | England |

**Model based on Trevithick's drawings of his steam train**

## Electric train

Although the first electric train had only a small locomotive and three carriages (it ran in a circle at a fair in Berlin, Germany), it paved the way for rapid improvements. By the mid-1880s, electric trains were operating in the USA, in Germany, and in the UK.

| | |
|---|---|
| **INVENTED BY** | Werner von Siemens |
| **WHEN** | 1879 |
| **WHERE** | Germany |

## Monorail

A single rail train, or monorail, first opened in England in the 1820s, but it depended on horsepower. The first successful powered monorail opened in Germany some 80 years later. It still operates today, and carries millions of passengers each year. It is known as the Wuppertal Suspension Railway.

**INVENTED BY** Eugen Langen

**WHEN** 1901

**WHERE** Germany

**The Wuppertal Suspension Railway**

## Maglev (magnetic levitation)

These trains use magnets to lift and drive a train forwards. Maglev technology has been developed by a number of people, but the world's first passenger-carrying maglev opened in 1984.

**INVENTED BY** Eric Laithwaite

**WHEN** 1984

**WHERE** England

**Modern-day maglev, Shanghai, China**

# Air and space

We are used to seeing aeroplanes in our skies and hearing of unmanned probes heading into deep space, but the first aeroplane only took off just over one hundred years ago.

FOCUS ON...
**FUN IN THE AIR**
Today's versions of some inventions have come a long way.

### Hot-air balloon

The first creatures to fly in a hot-air balloon were a duck, a cockerel, and a sheep. The balloon was made from paper and fabric and it flew for eight minutes. This replica of the world's first balloon, the "Montgolfier", was built for a show in Poland.

**INVENTED BY** Montgolfier brothers
**WHEN** 1783
**WHERE** France

### Aeroplane

An aeroplane called *The Flyer* made history when its pilot achieved the first controlled, powered flight in 1903. It rose to a height of about 3 m (10 ft) and flew about 37 m (120 ft) – that's a little less than the length of a jumbo jet. The flight lasted 12 seconds.

The Flyer *had a wooden frame*

◀ The first recorded parachute jump was made by Louis-Sebastién Lenormand in France in 1783.

◀ Russian inventor Aleksandr F Andreyev sketched ideas for a jet pack as long ago as 1919. This jet pack flew in 2008.

◀ Hang gliding took off in the 1970s with the delta wing, but the first glider took off in the 1850s.

**INVENTED BY** Wilbur and Orville Wright

**WHEN** 1903

**WHERE** USA

*The elevator tipped the plane up or down*

## Helicopter

Although previous helicopter designs had been tested, the first practical single rotor helicopter was known as the VS 300. It became the first production helicopter. This famous photograph shows its inventor Igor Sikorsky flying the machine – its first flight was a tethered flight (it was attached to the ground with a cable).

**INVENTED BY** Igor Sikorsky

**WHEN** 1940

**WHERE** Russia/USA

## Rocket

The first rockets were simple fireworks, dependent on solid fuel. Liquid fuel was first used in the 1920s, when Robert Goddard designed a rocket fuelled by a mixture of petrol and liquid oxygen.

**INVENTED BY**
Robert Goddard

**WHEN** 1926

**WHERE**
USA

## Satellite

Many artificial satellites orbit Earth, transmitting data. The first artificial satellite, *Sputnik 1*, was launched by the Soviet Union. It was the size of a large beach ball.

**INVENTED BY**
Soviet team led by Mikhail Tikhonravov

**WHEN** 1957

**WHERE**
Soviet Union

**Model of *Sputnik 1***

## Lunar Roving Vehicle (LRV)

Also known as the moon buggy, the first LRV was used on the Moon in 1971 as a part of the *Apollo 15* mission. It was the result of years of research and development in the 1960s by huge teams of people. However, the key design work is credited to a Filipino engineer, Eduardo San Juan.

**INVENTED BY** NASA

**WHEN** 1971

**WHERE** USA

## Space Shuttle

The Space Shuttle carried the world's first reusable spacecraft, the Orbiter. The Shuttle consisted of three main parts: a winged Orbiter, two white booster rockets, and a huge fuel tank. Equipment was carried into space in a large payload bay.

*Fuel tank*

**INVENTED BY** NASA

**WHEN** 1981

**WHERE** USA

Discovery was one of five Orbiters

USA
NASA
Discovery

Booster rocket

## Manned Manoeuvring Unit

This handy suit, known as an MMU, allowed an astronaut to go on spacewalks without having to be tethered to their spacecraft. The suits were last used in 1984.

**INVENTED BY** Martin Marietta Corporation

**WHEN** 1978

**WHERE** USA

## Mars exploration rover

Two rovers, *Spirit* and *Opportunity*, landed on Mars in 2004 and set off to explore a tiny part of the planet's surface. *Opportunity* continues to send back data, but *Spirit* stopped transmitting in 2011.

**INVENTED BY** NASA

**WHEN** 2003

**WHERE** USA

**BEYOND THE
SOLAR SYSTEM**
The twin craft *Voyager
1* and *Voyager 2* were
launched by NASA in
1977 to study the giant
planets of the Solar
System. They flew past
Jupiter and Saturn,
and *Voyager 2* also
passed Uranus and
Neptune, reaching
Neptune in 1989.
*Voyager 1* has now
left the Solar System.

At more than

# 17 billion km

(10.5 billion miles) from the Sun, *Voyager 1* is the farthest human-made object from Earth

# Navigational tools

It's good to travel somewhere, but you need to know where you are going. A number of important inventions have helped people to avoid getting lost, whether on land or navigating at sea.

## Magnetic compass

The first compasses to use needles to point north appeared in Europe in around 1100. Long before that, the Chinese had discovered that a suspended piece of lodestone points north. Lodestone is a magnetic rock.

**INVENTED BY**  Unknown

**WHEN**  c.500

**WHERE**  China

*This ancient Chinese compass, used a magnetic stone "spoon"*

## Octant

This piece of equipment was invented at a similar time but independently in the USA and England. It enabled sailors to find their exact position at sea by using the Sun, Moon, and stars. A later version, the sextant, provided more accuracy. Most octants were made of wood and ivory.

**INVENTED BY**  John Hadley (England) and Thomas Godfrey (USA)

**WHEN**  c.1730

**WHERE**  England and USA

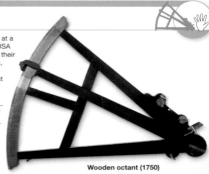

**Wooden octant (1750)**

## Sextant

The sextant was developed from the octant, but was more accurate. Sextants were made of brass. The first was suggested by Scottish-born John Campbell and made up two years later by John Bird. Many sailors still use sextants for navigation at sea.

*A sextant in use*

**INVENTED BY**
John Campbell
**WHEN** 1757
**WHERE** Scotland

## Marine chronometer

After its invention, this became an essential tool for ships (until the invention of GPS) as it enabled sailors to know exactly where they were in terms of longitude (their east-west position on the Earth's surface).

**INVENTED BY**
John Harrison
**WHEN** 1761
**WHERE**
England

## GPS

*GPS screen*

Global Positioning Systems (GPS) were first developed for the US air force in the 1970s. They work by linking up to different satellites to establish the receiver's location.

**INVENTED BY** Roger L Easton, Sr.
**WHEN** 1978
**WHERE** USA

# Everyday inventions

Thinking about a world without inventions would be to imagine a much more difficult daily existence. We depend on inventions to keep us safer and help make our lives easier or more comfortable, whether they are objects in the home or the materials your home or school are made from.

**TYPEWRITER**
The invention of the typewriter in 1874 and, more importantly, its keyboard layout, led to the computer keyboards we use today.

# Round the clock

From the time we get up to when we climb into bed, most of us will use certain inventions during the day. You probably use a toothbrush, and wash with soap. You may well glance in a mirror, checking your clothes. Take a look at some of the inventions we use daily.

## Paying for goods

If you're out and about, you may need to buy something. Money was invented for times when people had no goods to trade. Credit and debit cards mean that people don't need to carry cash. The first cards appeared in the early 1950s.

## Clothing

Fitted clothing dates back at least to the invention of the needle. Bone needles have been found that are at least 60,000 years old. Their appearance meant that clothes could be shaped around the body.

**Ancient Roman bone needles**

# I see you!

Glasses to correct vision are an invention that has benefited millions of people. Spectacles were first used more than 700 years ago. Early spectacles were pivoted to grip the nose.

**Pivoted spectacles**

# Let's eat!

All sorts of inventions help us in preparing the food we eat, but perhaps the most important (and useful) of these is the knife.

**Range of knives**

# A comfortable home

The invention of electric lighting brought a huge change to people's lives. Inventions such as heaters and cooling fans (depending on local weather conditions) have also helped with comfort in the home.

The radiator was invented to heat a home in the 1850s

Small tables were being used in ancient Egypt 5,300 years ago

FOCUS ON...
## HYGIENE
It's good to keep clean, whether it's washing your hands before a meal or taking a bath or shower. Many inventions help us to keep clean.

◀ Flushing toilets existed in many ancient civilizations, though they were more basic than those we enjoy today.

▲ Soap was invented by the Babylonians around 2800 BCE. However, their soap was made from fat and ashes.

▲ The first liquid shampoo didn't appear until 1927 – before that, people used soap.

# In the home
Many of the items you use every day were invented within the last 200 years. However, some may surprise you as they date back considerably further. One of the most commonly used items, the mirror, has a particularly ancient history.

**Mirror**

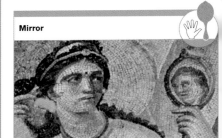

The practice of checking our reflections goes back a long way; the first mirrors dating back some 8,000 years. These mirrors were discs of polished stone. Craftsmen then began to use copper and, a little later, bronze as a reflective surface. The first glass mirrors appeared in Italy about 800 years ago.

| | |
|---|---|
| **INVENTED BY** | Unknown |
| **WHEN** | c.6000 BCE |
| **WHERE** | Unknown |

## Scissors

Scissors designed with two blades that pivot at the centre were invented by the ancient Romans, though spring scissors (connected at the handle) had been used long before that. Today there is a huge variety of specialist scissors, for tasks from dressmaking to surgery.

**INVENTED BY** Ancient Romans

**WHEN** 100 CE

**WHERE** Italy

## Light bulb

The light bulb was actually invented independently in the USA and in England in the same year. One of the trickiest bits was finding a suitable filament (the bit that glows).

Filament

**INVENTED BY** Joseph Swann (England) and Thomas Edison (USA)

**WHEN** 1878

**WHERE** England and USA

Replica of Edison's lamp

## Toothpaste in a tube

The first successful toothpaste in a tube was made by William Colgate, a New York soap and candle maker. He called it "Ribbon Dental Cream". However, an American dentist, Washington Sheffield, made an earlier version.

**INVENTED BY** Washington Sheffield

**WHEN** 1892

**WHERE** USA

## Sewing machine

Like many inventions, a successful sewing machine was the result of a number of different inventions, each an improvement on the last. Two of the key contributors were Americans Elias Howe and Isaac Singer.

**INVENTED BY**
Walter Hunt, Elias Howe, Isaac Singer

**WHEN** 1846

**WHERE** USA

Sewing machine (1850s)

## Vacuum cleaner

The first vacuum cleaner was so large it had to be pulled up to a house by a horse. The machine itself was fuelled by petrol. Apparently it was so noisy that it scared any passing horses!

**INVENTED BY**
Hubert Cecil Booth

**WHEN** 1901

**WHERE** England

## Dishwasher

The first practical dishwasher was hand powered. It was invented by a woman who wanted to find a way to stop her china being chipped when it was washed by hand. The one shown here was advertised as cleaning dishes in just two minutes.

**INVENTED BY** Josephine Cochran

**WHEN** 1886

**WHERE** USA

Dishwasher (1920s)

## Toaster

Toast was enjoyed in ancient Rome when bread was held in front of a fire to heat it. The first electric toaster was invented in the 1890s, but its wiring tended to melt so it wasn't popular.

**INVENTED BY**
Alan MacMasters
**WHEN** 1893
**WHERE**
Scotland

**Toaster (1914)**

## Washing machine

A drum washing machine was patented by James King in 1851, but it was hand powered. The first electric powered washing machine didn't appear until the early 1900s. This machine, made in 1929, was one of the most popular of early American washing machine brands, a Thor.

**INVENTED BY**
Unknown
**WHEN** 1906
**WHERE** USA

## Ink

Ink has been used for around 4,500 years, and we now depend on it for all sorts of uses, from art and design to books to food labelling. The first inks were made from solid blocks, which had to be wetted. They were made from soot mixed with glue.

| | |
|---|---|
| **INVENTED BY** | Chinese |
| **WHEN** | c.2500 BCE |
| **WHERE** | China |

Solid inks are still used by artists

## Pencil

An early form of a pencil was made in the 1500s when graphite was placed in a wooden holder (it was too soft to use on its own). The graphite was mistakenly called lead; we still sometimes refer to pencils as lead pencils though there's no lead in them. Today, pencils contain a mixture of graphite and clay.

| | |
|---|---|
| **INVENTED BY** | Conrad Gesner |
| **WHEN** | 1565 |
| **WHERE** | England |

## Paperclip

A paperclip machine was patented in 1899 by American William Middlebrook but it's thought that the clips themselves, also known as Gem clips, had probably been invented some time earlier.

| | |
|---|---|
| **INVENTED BY** | Unknown |
| **WHEN** | 1890s |
| **WHERE** | Unknown |

Metal paperclips with plastic coat

## Adhesive tape

Rolls of sticky tape are widely used for wrapping parcels. This tape originated because there was a need to stick together pieces of cellophane, a transparent film used to wrap food in the 1920s. The result was Scotch tape (this name is still used in the USA and Canada). In 1937, Sellotape, a similar item, was first produced in Britain.

**INVENTED BY** Richard Drew
**WHEN** 1930
**WHERE** USA

## Ballpoint pen

An early version of the ballpoint pen appeared in 1888, invented by American John Loud. However, his ballpoint didn't take off. That happened 30 years later when the ballpoint pen was invented by the Hungarian painter and journalist Laszlo Jozsef Biro.

**INVENTED BY** Laszlo Biro
**WHEN** 1938
**WHERE** Hungary

**Biro (1945)**

## Sticky notes

These notes came about after Spencer Silver discovered a mildly sticky glue. His colleague, Art Fry, suggested they try it on the paper notes that he used to mark pages in his music book. "Post-it" notes now come in a variety of designs.

**INVENTED BY** Spencer Silver and Art Fry
**WHEN** 1980
**WHERE** USA

# Measuring instruments

Ancient people developed a number of ways of measuring time, length, and weight. The ability to measure accurately is important in industries from building to dressmaking. Global industries depend on accurate measurement: car parts, for example, are made all over the world, yet come together to fit perfectly.

## Sundial

The ability to tell the time from the shadow the Sun casts dates back to ancient times. The ancient Egyptians used sundials 3,500 years ago, but they were probably invented long before this.

**INVENTED BY**  Unknown

**WHEN**  At least 1500 BCE

**WHERE**  Unknown

*The part of a sundial that casts a shadow is called the gnomon*

Shadow

## Water clock

A water clock measures time by the slow release of water. Nobody really knows when and where they were invented, but they are thought to be one of the oldest of all measuring devices. One water clock was found in the tomb of an ancient Egyptian pharaoh.

**INVENTED BY**  Unknown

**WHEN**  c.1500 BCE

**WHERE**  Unknown

**Illustration of a water clock from ancient Greece**

## Sand glass

A sand glass (or hour glass) is another device for measuring time. The sand flows through a narrow hole from one glass bulb to another, taking a certain amount of time to do so.

**INVENTED BY**
Unknown
**WHEN** c.300 CE
**WHERE** Unknown

## Pendulum clock

A pendulum is a swinging weight. Its addition to a clock made time keeping more accurate than previously. The pendulum clock was designed by a Dutchman called Huygens and built to his design by a clockmaker.

Longcase pendulum clocks are often called "Grandfather clocks" ... but nobody knows why!

**INVENTED BY**
Christiaan Huygens
**WHEN** 1656
**WHERE**
The Netherlands

## Quartz clock

Today, most clocks and watches contain a tiny quartz crystal. The use of quartz was a major development in time keeping, as it results in a more accurate clock than one driven by a pendulum. Unlike pendulum clocks, quartz clocks and watches don't need winding up.

**INVENTED BY**
Warren Marrison and J W Horton at Bell Telephone Laboratories
**WHEN** 1927
**WHERE** USA

## Weighing scales

If you bake, it helps to weigh your ingredients. The first set of scales was a simple invention. Known as a beam balance, it had a rod that held a pan at each end. The first weights were probably made from stones.

**INVENTED BY**
Unknown
**WHEN** c.4000 BCE
**WHERE**
Mesopotamia
(modern-day Iraq)

## Spirit level

Carpenters still use spirit levels to ensure something is lying straight. Spirit levels use a bubble in liquid to show an accurate horizontal line. They were invented hundreds of years ago.

**INVENTED BY** Melchisédech Thévenot
**WHEN** 1661
**WHERE** France

STABILA ■ Laser S
70L

## Calendar

The first calendars charted the movements of the Moon and the Sun, but were not particularly accurate. Calendars based solely on the Sun's movements appeared in ancient Egyptian times. This is an ancient Babylonian astronomical calendar.

**INVENTED BY**
Babylonians
**WHEN** c.3000 BCE
**WHERE** Mesopotamia
(modern-day Iraq)

Stream
of atoms
produced here

The first spirit levels (or "bubble rules") were used on telescopes. They were used by carpenters much later.

**Laser spirit level**

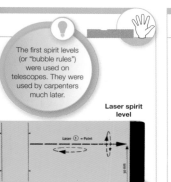

Laser ① = Point

## Measuring tape

A flexible ruler is a useful tool. Before rulers and tape measures were invented, people had used chain, rope, and even strips of leather to measure length. The first spring tape measure was patented by Alvin J Fellows, though it was an improvement on earlier designs.

| INVENTED BY | Alvin J Fellows |
| WHEN | 1868 |
| WHERE | USA |

## Atomic clock

The first atomic clock, shown here, was calculated to be so accurate that it would gain or lose no more than one second every 300 years. It worked using the vibrations created by atoms. Atomic clocks remain the most accurate of all clocks.

| INVENTED BY | Louis Essen and Jack Parry |
| WHEN | 1955 |
| WHERE | England |

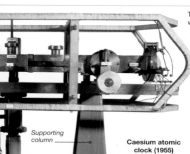

Supporting column

**Caesium atomic clock (1955)**

# Clothing

It's thought that people first wore clothes some 170,000 years ago. These would have been animal hides draped around the body as the needle was a much later invention.

FOCUS ON...
**FASTENINGS**
How are your clothes held together? The fastenings we use are relatively recent inventions.

---

### Shoes

The first shoes to enclose the feet were made of soft leather pulled around the ankles with a thong. Before this, people had worn open-toed sandals. Today there exists an enormous variety of different footwear.

**INVENTED BY** Unknown

**WHEN** c.1500 BCE

**WHERE** Mesopotamia (modern-day Iraq)

Adidas sports shoes

*Screw-in studs were invented in the 1920s*

---

### Raincoat

A patent for combining rubber and fabric to make a waterproof material was taken out by Charles Macintosh in the 1800s. He went on to make the first Macintosh waterproof coats. The early fabric had problems, as it melted in hot weather and, apparently, was rather smelly!

**INVENTED BY** Charles Macintosh

**WHEN** 1823

**WHERE** Scotland

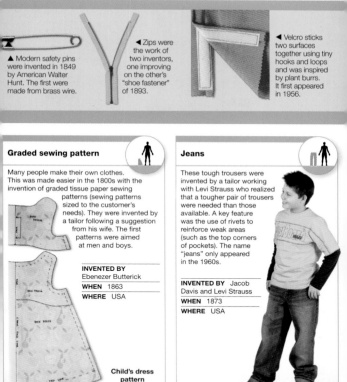

▲ Modern safety pins were invented in 1849 by American Walter Hunt. The first were made from brass wire.

◀ Zips were the work of two inventors, one improving on the other's "shoe fastener" of 1893.

◀ Velcro sticks two surfaces together using tiny hooks and loops and was inspired by plant burrs. It first appeared in 1956.

## Graded sewing pattern

Many people make their own clothes. This was made easier in the 1800s with the invention of graded tissue paper sewing patterns (sewing patterns sized to the customer's needs). They were invented by a tailor following a suggestion from his wife. The first patterns were aimed at men and boys.

**INVENTED BY** Ebenezer Butterick

**WHEN** 1863

**WHERE** USA

Child's dress pattern

## Jeans

These tough trousers were invented by a tailor working with Levi Strauss who realized that a tougher pair of trousers were needed than those available. A key feature was the use of rivets to reinforce weak areas (such as the top corners of pockets). The name "jeans" only appeared in the 1960s.

**INVENTED BY** Jacob Davis and Levi Strauss

**WHEN** 1873

**WHERE** USA

**COTTON**
Woven from thin cotton threads, cotton fabric wrinkles easily. The invention of nylon and polyester in the 1930s caused the cotton industry to suffer because clothes made from synthetic fibres didn't need ironing. However, in the 1950s a chemist called Ruth Benerito created wrinkle-free cotton, an invention of immense value.

The invention of
wrinkle-free
cotton saved the
# cotton
# industry

# Materials

The synthetic, or man-made, materials we use in our everyday lives make our lives more comfortable. Cement and steel strengthen the buildings in which many people live. Plastics, invented in the nineteenth century, are now one of the most widely used of all synthetic materials.

### Portland cement

Cement has been used for thousands of years as a bonding substance for building work. Today, the world's most widely used cement is called Portland Cement, yet it was only created some 200 years ago.

| | |
|---|---|
| **INVENTED BY** | Joseph Aspdin |
| **WHEN** | 1824 |
| **WHERE** | England |

*Cement is added to gravel, sand, and water to make concrete*

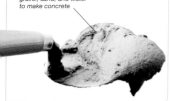

### Vulcanized rubber

The strengthened (or "vulcanized") rubber used for items such as bicycle and car tyres was developed in the 1830s (though a form of vulcanized rubber had been used in Mesoamerica (modern-day Central America) some 3,600 years ago). The first car tyres were white. Black tyres emerged later. Most tyres are black because of the carbon added to them when they are made, chosen because it makes the tyres stronger.

| | |
|---|---|
| **INVENTED BY** | Charles Goodyear |
| **WHEN** | 1839 |
| **WHERE** | USA |

*Treads help a car grip the road*

## Plastics: Celluloid

There is an amazing variety of plastics, with different strengths and properties. The first usable plastic was celluloid, and it was used for making billiard balls. Unfortunately they had a tendency to explode on impact! Modern billiard balls are made from a plastic that is resistant to cracking.

**INVENTED BY** John Wesley Hyatt

**WHEN** 1869

**WHERE** USA

## Plastics: Polythene

Polythene is now the world's most commonly produced plastic (PVC is the second). It is used for all sorts of plastic bags, including supermarket carriers, sandwich bags, and freezer bags. Yet the first consumer product to be made out of polythene (in 1948) wasn't a plastic bag – it was a washing-up bowl.

**INVENTED BY** Eric Fawcett and Reginald Gibson

**WHEN** 1933

**WHERE** England

*Food is kept fresh* _____

## Stainless steel

Steel was discovered when people combined iron and charcoal. Stainless steel was discovered when chromium was added to ordinary steel. The wonder of stainless steel is the fact that it is long lasting and doesn't need constant maintenance. Its inventor named it "rustless steel" and realised that it was perfect for cutlery.

**INVENTED BY**
Harry Brearley
**WHEN**
1913
**WHERE**
England

## Kevlar

This is an incredibly strong plastic that can be spun and woven into fabric – it is the material used for bullet-proof vests. Kevlar is also resistant to heat and to corrosive liquids, so is ideal for use in firefighter's suits. In fact, it has five times the strength of steel.

**INVENTED BY**
Stephanie Kwolek,
Herbert Blades, Paul
Morgan
**WHEN** 1965
**WHERE** USA

## Float glass

The ancient Romans used glass, but the windows in today's buildings rely on a more recent invention, float glass. This is made by floating molten glass on a bed of molten metal, which automatically produces plate glass with a smooth surface. Before the invention of float glass, plate glass had to be polished smooth in a separate process, making it more expensive.

*Modern buildings make use of float glass*

**INVENTED BY** Alastair Pilkington

**WHEN** 1950s

**WHERE** England

## Glulam

Glued laminated timber, or Glulam, was an exciting invention as it changed the ways in which wood could be used. Basically, pieces of wood are glued together, meaning smaller pieces can be put together to create huge, structural buildings. Glulam structures are versatile, light, and very strong.

**INVENTED BY** Otto Hetzer

**WHEN** 1906

**WHERE** Germany

# Money

We all depend on money, with countries around the world having different currencies. There was a time, however, when people traded goods for goods (called bartering) and money did not exist.

## FOCUS ON...
### COUNTING
Traders have had to keep track of their goods for thousands of years. A number of ancient counting devices helped.

▲ The abacus has been called the fifth invention of China. The type shown was invented in the second century BCE.

▶ Handheld calculators appeared in the 1960s, able to calculate basic multiplication and division.

▲ Napier's bones was invented about 400 years ago and used for the multiplication of large numbers. Early versions used bones.

## Coins

Coins today are standard in terms of the sizing and metals used. It's thought that they were introduced in a number of different places around the same time, though the earliest coins were not of standard weights and sizes.

| | |
|---|---|
| **INVENTED BY** | Unknown |
| **WHEN** | c.700–600 BCE |
| **WHERE** | India, Lydia (now modern-day Turkey), China |

*Lydian coins, made of a mixture of gold and silver*

## Notes

Why use notes? Coins are heavy to carry and notes mean that larger amounts can be held with ease. Notes first appeared when banks guaranteed the amount printed on a piece of paper.

**INVENTED BY** Chinese

**WHEN** c.800 CE

**WHERE** China

## Bar code

Many shops depend on bar codes to identify their stock. The first bar code was devised after one of the inventors overheard a shop manager saying it would be good to have a way of identifying products at the checkout.

**INVENTED BY** Joseph Woodland and Bernard Silver

**WHEN** 1952

**WHERE** USA

All supermarket products have a bar code

## Automated teller machine

Automated teller machines (ATMs) are handy when people need money quickly. They can be used to transfer or withdraw money from a card holder's account. Shepherd-Barron's machine was the first to be installed, but James Goodfellow's invention read a card so was more similar to the machines we use today.

**INVENTED BY** John Shepherd-Barron and James Goodfellow

**WHEN** 1967

**WHERE** England

# Entertainment and culture

From enjoying a puppet show to learning to play a musical instrument, and from bouncing on a trampoline to visiting a theme park, we all like to have fun. We are surrounded by inventions that are designed to entertain, and many of them have older origins than you may think.

**BOWLING**
Many people enjoy ten-pin bowling. There is evidence that bowling was enjoyed more than 5,000 years ago in ancient Egypt.

# Time to relax

Some inventions are developed just for the purpose of having fun. From playing an instrument to watching a film, it's fun to have fun, and inventors are constantly producing new ideas for toys and entertainment.

### Theme parks

Amusement, or theme, parks grew in size as people looked for entertainment when they gathered at fairs. The first roller coaster to have cars fixed to a track opened in France in 1817. Today, high-speed roller coaster rides are very popular.

**Roller coaster** tracks are made from steel

# Puppets

Puppetry was popular in ancient times. Stick puppets were used in India 4,000 years ago and also in ancient Egypt. Puppet shows remain popular all over the world.

**Puppets at a show in Nepal**

# Making music

The discovery of ancient bone flutes, found in a cave in Germany in 2009, tells us that people have been making music for at least 40,000 years. There are now huge numbers of musical instruments that people can choose to learn.

**Modern drum kit**

## A WORLD OF TOYS

There is plenty of evidence that all sorts of simple toys were played with thousands of years ago, as they are today.

**Carved animals** have been found in Egypt's Nile Valley. They date back 3,000 years.

Nobody knows when the **ball** was invented. There are now a lot of different types, which has led to a huge variety of games.

**Lego®** was invented in 1949 and has become one of the most popular toys of all time.

# Music

Many people who play a musical instrument join a band or an orchestra. An orchestra is usually divided into four sections: brass, woodwind, strings, and percussion. Each section has a number of instruments that are defined by that label. Other instruments cannot be so easily categorized.

## Drum (percussion)

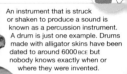

An instrument that is struck or shaken to produce a sound is known as a percussion instrument. A drum is just one example. Drums made with alligator skins have been dated to around 6000 BCE but nobody knows exactly when or where they were invented.

**INVENTED BY**  Unknown
**WHEN**  6000 BCE
**WHERE**  Unknown

Peruvian sculpture (c.800 CE)

## Flute (woodwind)

The oldest musical instruments that have been discovered are two bone flutes found in Germany. Flutes belong to the woodwind group of instruments, which also includes the oboe and clarinet. The modern flute, held sideways, is a much more recent invention, dating from around 200 BCE.

**INVENTED BY**  Unknown
**WHEN**  800 BCE
**WHERE**  Unknown

## Trumpet (brass)

One of three valves

The ancient Egyptians played trumpets, now a part of the brass section of an orchestra. However, early trumpets didn't have valves, which were added in the 1800s.

**INVENTED BY**  Unknown
**WHEN**  1500 BCE
**WHERE**  Unknown

## Violin (strings)

A violin belongs to the stringed family of instruments (a viola and a cello are other stringed instruments). The violin as used today originated in the 1500s in Italy. One of the first successful makers was an Italian craftsman called Andrea Amati.

*A bow is drawn over strings to create sound*

| INVENTED BY | Unknown |
| --- | --- |
| WHEN | 1530 |
| WHERE | Italy |

## Piano

The piano was invented because there was a need for an instrument similar to the harpsichord, but which responded more sensitively to the player's touch. A piano has keys that strike strings (not pluck them as with the harpsichord). The harder the keys are struck, the louder the sound. Pianos developed from earlier spinets (a type of harpsichord), such as this one.

Oval spinet, Bartolomeo Cristofori (1695)

| INVENTED BY | Bartolomeo Cristofori |
| --- | --- |
| WHEN | 1709 |
| WHERE | Italy |

# All things sound

It's common to see people listening to music or to radio broadcasts as they walk about. It's perhaps surprising that the inventions that led to this portable technology date back less than 150 years, and the first inventions in this area were far from portable.

## Phonograph

Thomas Edison made history when he wrapped tin foil around a rotating cylinder and recorded his voice using a needle to mark the vibrations on the tin foil. Others had done this, but his machine could then replay the sound.

**INVENTED BY** Thomas Edison
**WHEN** 1877
**WHERE** USA

## Microphone

In development, as shown below, this invention may not have looked much, but it was immensely important to the emergence of the telephone. The inventor was excited to discover that his device could pick up sounds otherwise hidden to the human ear.

**INVENTED BY**
David Hughes
**WHEN** 1878
**WHERE** England

Hughes demonstrated his microphone by using it to pick up the sounds of insects walking!

*Wire connects to earpiece*

## Gramophone

The invention of the gramophone was a terrific leap forwards as it used flat disc records rather than cylinders for the recorded sound. Flat discs were easier to mass produce. They quickly became popular among musicians wanting to record their music.

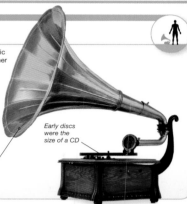

| | |
|---|---|
| **INVENTED BY** | Emile Berliner |
| **WHEN** | 1887 |
| **WHERE** | USA |

*Early discs were the size of a CD*

*A large horn was used to project the sound*

## Headphones

Many people use headphones to listen to music or while playing computer games. The first headphones were used by telephone operators in the 1880s, and they were heavy items. The first headphones to look something like those we use today appeared in 1910. Nowadays, there is a huge range on the market, from tiny ear buds to "noise-cancelling" headphones (designed to reduce outside noise).

| | |
|---|---|
| **INVENTED BY** | Nathaniel Baldwin |
| **WHEN** | 1910 |
| **WHERE** | USA |

Beats headphones (2008)

## RADIO
Radio broadcasts need no wires – they rely on signals that use invisible waves. Radio waves were discovered by German scientist, Henrich Hertz, in 1887, having been predicted by Scottish physicist James Clerk Maxwell in 1867. They were first put to use by Italian inventor Guglielmo Marconi in 1901.

# Radio waves travel at the
# speed of light –
### that's about 300,000 km (186,400 miles) a second.

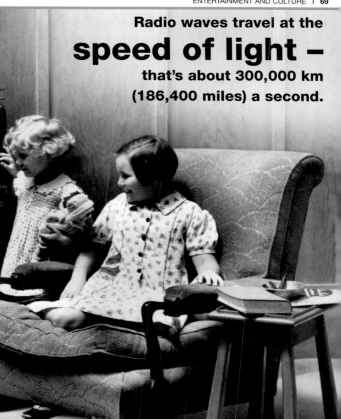

## Magnetic recording

A Danish telephone engineer invented a telephone answering machine, the telegraphone. By inventing this, he invented something new: magnetic recording. Messages were recorded on a reel of thin steel wire. It was a significant breakthrough in sound recording.

**INVENTED BY**
Valdemar Poulsen

**WHEN** 1898

**WHERE**
Denmark

## Long-playing record

The long-playing (LP) record was made of a bendy plastic, and allowed 25 minutes of recording on each side. Previous discs would break easily and only played for four minutes on each side. So the LPs were immensely popular.

**INVENTED BY** Peter Goldmark

**WHEN** 1948

**WHERE**
USA

## Digital audio player

Today, the most well known audio player is the iPod but the first audio player appeared in 1979. This prototype was the size of a credit card, and the inventor filed a patent for it in 1981. However, he failed to successfully develop it.

The first audio player could hold only 3.5 minutes of sound (though there were plans to extend this).

**INVENTED BY** Kane Kramer

**WHEN** 1979

**WHERE** England

## Walkman

The Walkman's inventor also gave it its name – he wanted a cassette player that was small enough to be carried. Initially it was known as the Soundabout in the USA and the Stowaway in the UK, but those names never caught on.

**INVENTED BY** Akio Morita

**WHEN** 1979

**WHERE** Japan

## Compact disc (CD)

Two huge companies worked together to invent the CD, although they were competitors. The first CD album (made just for demonstration in 1981) was *Living Eyes* by a band called the Bee Gees.

**INVENTED BY** Philips Electronics and Sony Corporation

**WHEN** 1982

**WHERE** The Netherlands and Japan

# Cinema

Thousands of films are released every year and a trip to the cinema is a popular outing. We watch films in cinemas, projected onto enormous outdoor screens, and on hand-held devices. The development of the film industry has seen a number of key inventions over the past 100 years or so.

### Cinématographe

The idea of an audience sitting together to watch a film owes its origins to two brothers and their cinématographe. This machine acted as a camera and projector to show an audience a moving picture that had been recorded on to a continuous strip of film. The first films were short (and silent) but they captivated audiences.

**INVENTED BY** Auguste and Louis Lumière
**WHEN** 1895
**WHERE** France

Lens for projecting images on to a large screen

A cinématographe could be moved to take a film to an audience

# Kinetoscope

This machine worked by moving a sequence of photographs (40 per second) past a shutter. The shutter opened briefly, allowing light to flash through each image, and the user saw a moving image. However, a kinetoscope could be used by just one person at a time.

| | |
|---|---|
| **INVENTED BY** | William Dickson |
| **WHEN** | 1893 |
| **WHERE** | USA |

A kinetoscope film lasted just 20 seconds.

# Cinemascope

As film-making became more widespread, one problem became apparent. The film that was shot had a trimmed effect when projected onto cinema screens. The answer came with the cinemascope, which squeezed a wide image onto a normal film.

**INVENTED BY**
Henri Chrétien and
Claude Autant-Lara

**WHEN** 1928

**WHERE**
France

Henri Chrétien

# Camcorder

The invention of camcorders meant people could easily record their own films at family events (although the first camcorder was too bulky for home use). This was a device that combined a video camera and a video recorder.

| | |
|---|---|
| **INVENTED BY** | Sony Corporation |
| **WHEN** | 1983 |
| **WHERE** | Japan |

Camcorder (no longer widely used)

# Food and drink

Many of the things we eat and drink are grown on farms, but some cannot be grown – they were invented or discovered by combining different ingredients in a certain way.

## FOCUS ON...
## STORING FOOD

As populations grew, it became necessary to find better ways of keeping food.

▲ Canning emerged in France in 1809 with jars and with tin-coated iron.

▲ Refrigerators, first patented in 1851, are a useful means of keeping food cold.

### Leavened bread

Bread was eaten many thousands of years ago, but leavened bread (which uses a raising agent such as yeast) first appeared around 4,600 years ago. Today there are a huge variety of breads on the market, including breads with added fruits, seeds, and nuts.

| | |
|---|---|
| **INVENTED BY** | Ancient Egyptians |
| **WHEN** | 2600 BCE |
| **WHERE** | Egypt |

Holes in bread are caused by rising yeast

## Condensed milk

This invention came about when its inventor realized how many children were taken ill after drinking milk that had been infected with bacteria. The milk was boiled under vacuum, which sterilized and thickened it. It could then be safely canned for later use.

**INVENTED BY** Gail Borden

**WHEN** 1856

**WHERE** USA

## Coca-Cola

This popular drink was invented around 130 years ago by a pharmacist. For the first 17 years after its appearance, the ingredients included the drug cocaine (extracted from coca plants) and caffeine from kola nuts.

*The Coca-Cola logo is known throughout the world*

**INVENTED BY** John Pemberton

**WHEN** 1886

**WHERE** USA

## Tea bag

Although tea has been enjoyed for thousands of years, the idea of putting a little in a bag to brew is relatively recent. It's thought to have been an accidental invention by a tea shop owner who sent samples out in cloth bags.

**INVENTED BY** Thomas Sullivan

**WHEN** 1908

**WHERE** USA

*Tea in porous bag*

## Instant noodles

The first instant noodles were sold in Japan. They were chicken flavoured. In 1971 they reached a wider audience with the launch of a cup in which they could be mixed with hot water. Billions of these pot noodles have been sold.

**INVENTED BY** Momofuku Ando

**WHEN** 1958

**WHERE** Japan

Chocolate comes from the cacao tree. The Latin name of this tree is *Theobroma cacao*. "Theobroma" means "food of the gods".

### CHOCOLATE
Chocolate has been popular for thousands of years, but as a bitter tasting drink and not as a bar. The first bar of chocolate (as we would recognize it) appeared in 1847 in England. These bars had a gritty texture, but some were produced with fruit-flavoured centres – a form of chocolate still enjoyed today.

# Playtime

Children have always played with toys (as have adults!). It's thought the oldest toys were carved wooden dolls and animals. Over the years, many toys have emerged as the result of accidental discovery.

FOCUS ON...
**EARLY GAMES**
Two-player board games have a long history. Some are still played today.

## Yo-yo

The yo-yo is a widely used toy with ancient origins. Yo-yos were used in China some 4,000 years ago, and were pictured in art from ancient Greece some 2,500 years ago. Nobody is sure where the name "yo-yo" originated.

| | |
|---|---|
| **INVENTED BY** | Unknown |
| **WHEN** | Unknown |
| **WHERE** | Unknown |

## Trampoline

The first trampoline was simply a canvas stretched across a steel frame. It was called a bouncing rig. The inventor perfected it over a number of years, eventually using nylon webbing rather than canvas and adding springs. The name "trampoline" dates from 1937.

| | |
|---|---|
| **INVENTED BY** | George Nissen |
| **WHEN** | 1934 |
| **WHERE** | USA |

▲ Senet was played in Egypt more than 5,000 years ago. The original rules have been lost but versions are still played.

▲ Go is believed to have originated in China some 3,000 years ago.

▲ Chess, like Senet and Go, is a game for two players. It dates back to sixth-century India.

## Slinky

A slinky is a coiled spring that can "walk" down stairs. It proved an immensely popular toy after its release. It was an accidental invention – the inventor was actually trying to find ways of suspending sensitive equipment on ships.

| INVENTED BY | Richard T James |
| --- | --- |
| WHEN | 1945 |
| WHERE | USA |

## Rubik's cube

The first Rubik's cube was known as the "magic" cube but it was renamed (after its inventor) in 1980. It's believed that one in seven people around the world have played with a Rubik's cube.

| INVENTED BY | Ernö Rubik |
| --- | --- |
| WHEN | 1974 |
| WHERE | Hungary |

## Joystick

A joystick is a way in which people can control gaming movements on a computer console, but it was originally devised for use in aircraft in the early 1900s. The mechanical joystick used in aircraft bears little resemblance to that used for computer games.

**INVENTED BY**
C B Mirick

**WHEN** 1926

**WHERE** USA

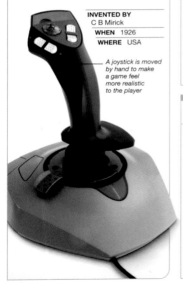

*A joystick is moved by hand to make a game feel more realistic to the player*

## View-Master

The View-Master was originally planned as an educational tool for adults, to show 3-D versions of objects. It was also a hit with children, and it's still in use more than 75 years after its first appearance.

**INVENTED BY**
William Gruber

**WHEN** 1938

**WHERE** USA

## Home video games

An engineer called Ralph Baer began to explore ways of using televisions to play games at home in the 1960s. The first home video game system was the result – the Magnavox Odyssey. Baer is known as the "father of the video game".

**INVENTED BY**
Ralph Baer

**WHEN** 1972

**WHERE** USA

## PlayStation

Only 200 units of the first PlayStation were made (in 1991) but it was hugely successful and became the best-selling gaming console of the 1990s. It was released under a team at Sony led by Ken Kutaragi.

**INVENTED BY** Sony

**WHEN** 1991

**WHERE** Japan

**Original PlayStation console**

## Xbox

As with all successful gaming consoles, there are now a series of Xbox consoles, but the original Xbox appeared in 2001. One million were sold in the three weeks after release.

**INVENTED BY** Microsoft

**WHEN** 2001

**WHERE** USA

## Nintendo Wii

The Wii brought together a number of different technologies; in effect, it was invented by a team of people. The "ii" in the name is said to represent players standing side by side, while Nintendo also explained that "Wii" sounds like "we". They promoted it as a gaming console for everyone to enjoy.

**INVENTED BY** Nintendo

**WHEN** 2006

**WHERE** Japan

*Wii hand-held controller*

# Medical marvels

Medical discoveries and inventions have allowed huge advances in the ability of doctors to cure their patients from injuries and diseases that would once have been incurable, and also to help them lead the life they want. Here, American paralympian Roderick Green leaps to win a bronze medal in the men's long jump at the Paralympics Summer Games in Australia in 2000.

**NEED A PLASTER?**
The first sticking plaster (named Band-Aid®) was invented in 1920 in the USA, developed by Earle Dickson for his wife.

# Inventions for health

About 1,000 years ago an encyclopedia of medical knowledge, *The Canon of Medicine,* sought to describe the causes of disease. It prompted a growing desire to help recovery from illness. This desire has led to a wealth of medical inventions.

### Kill those germs

The eventual understanding that germs spread disease helped medical progress. The discovery of antiseptics helped here as they kill germs. The first person to clean wounds with antiseptic was British surgeon Joseph Lister in the 1860s. He developed a "donkey engine", which sprayed a fine mist of antiseptic.

**Three robotic** arms are used for certain operations. One is a camera.

**Replica of Lister's "donkey engine"**

### Staying alive

Large hospitals have intensive care units, fitted with high-tech life support machinery. One of the first life support machines was the iron lung, the first practical one invented in 1928 by Philip Drinker. It breathed for the patient, if they were unable to do so, until their strength returned.

**Hand cranked** leather forge bellows mounted on wooden patient's chamber

**Early attempt at an iron lung**

## THE POWER OF PLANTS

Herbs have been used as medicines for thousands of years. Many modern medicines are based on plants.

**Sage**
is one of the most valuable of all herbs. It can even be used to fight memory loss.

**Mint**
is known to sooth headaches and fight feelings of sickness.

**Aloe**
plants are known for the soothing properties of their sap on sunburn.

## Robot help

The first use of a robotic arm to help in surgery took place in Vancouver, Canada, in 1983. Hundreds of thousands of operations are now carried out with the help of robots each year. These machines can grip, cut, and drill with more accuracy than a human hand.

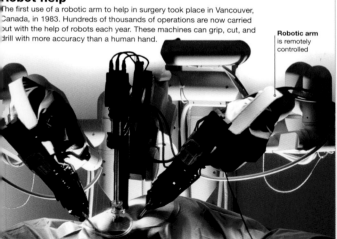

**Robotic arm**
is remotely controlled

▲ Penicillin, the first antibiotic, was discovered (not invented) by Alexander Fleming in 1928.

▲ Quinine, a treatment for malaria, occurs in the bark of the cinchona tree.

◄ Nystatin helps to prevent the spread of fungus (shown on this orange).

Treated area

# Medical aids

Some ingenious inventions allow doctors to find out exactly what is going on inside the human body without having to operate. Others help with specific problems once a diagnosis is made.

### Ultrasound scanner

An ultrasound scanner works by sending sound waves into a patient's body that then echo off bone or muscle. Different tissues produce different echos and these are used by the scanner to build up a picture.

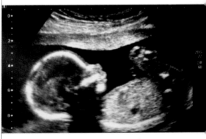

| INVENTED BY | Ian Donald, J MacVicar, T G Brown |
|---|---|
| **WHEN** | 1958 |
| **WHERE** | England |

## Fibre-optic endoscope

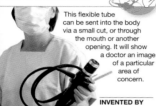

This flexible tube can be sent into the body via a small cut, or through the mouth or another opening. It will show a doctor an image of a particular area of concern.

**INVENTED BY**
Basil Hirschowitz and Larry Curtiss

**WHEN** 1957

**WHERE** USA

## CT scanner

CT (computerized tomography) scanning is used to build up cross-sectional pictures of the inside of a patient's body through the use of X-rays. The scanning machine has a large ring, and the patient is moved through the ring, stopping where the scan is needed.

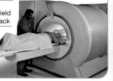

**INVENTED BY**
Godfrey Hounsfield and Allan Cormack

**WHEN** 1972

**WHERE**
UK and USA

## MRI scanner

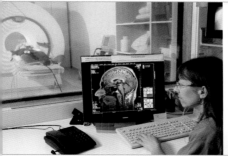

Magnetic Resonance Imaging (MRI) scanners provide an incredibly detailed way of seeing what is going on inside the body. They do this by using magnets and radio waves. The picture is produced on a computer and looks as if a "sliced" photograph has been taken across the body.

**INVENTED BY**
Raymond Damadian and Paul Lauterbur

**WHEN** 1977

**WHERE** USA

## Prosthetic (artificial limb)

The first artificial body part we know of is a wooden toe, found on an Egyptian mummy and estimated to date back 2,700–3,000 years. It was attached to the foot with a leather strap.

**INVENTED BY**
Unknown

**WHEN** 1000 BCE

**WHERE** Unknown

Wooden toe

## Clinical thermometer

It's now common practice to check a patient's temperature (a healthy human body temperature is about 37°C/98.6°F). However, this did not become common until the early 1900s. The first modern mercury thermometer was invented by the person who later introduced the Fahrenheit temperature scale. The clinical thermometer was invented some time later.

**INVENTED BY**
Thomas Allbutt

**WHEN** 1866

**WHERE**
England

The mercury level shows temperature after it is removed from the patient

## Stethoscope

A stethoscope allows a doctor to listen to the sounds inside a person's body, such as their heartbeat, breathing, and even blood flow. The first stethoscope was a simple wooden tube.

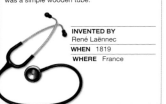

**INVENTED BY**
René Laënnec

**WHEN** 1819

**WHERE** France

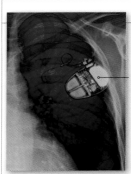

Pacemaker as seen on a coloured X-ray

## Blood pressure monitor

Blood pressure is a good indication of a person's health and a means of measuring it first appeared with the sphygmomanometer. The name originates from two Greek words and means "measurement of the pulse".

| INVENTED BY | Samuel von Basch |
|---|---|
| WHEN | 1881 |
| WHERE | Austria |

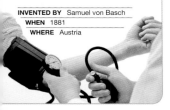

## Pacemaker

If a person's heart is damaged and cannot beat properly, a pacemaker can regulate it. The first pacemaker was the size of a toaster and had to be plugged into a wall socket. A pacemaker small enough to wear on the body appeared five years later.

| INVENTED BY | Earl Bakken |
|---|---|
| WHEN | 1957 |
| WHERE | USA |

Different sources have been used to power pacemakers over the years, including plutonium-238 (a radioactive material).

## Apgar newborn test

This test provides a fast way of checking a newborn baby's wellbeing using a scoring system, so that help can be given quickly if needed. The score ranges from 0 to 10 and looks at five things: appearance, pulse, grimace, activity, and respiration. Its widespread introduction resulted in many lives being saved.

| INVENTED BY | Virginia Apgar |
|---|---|
| WHEN | 1952 |
| WHERE | USA |

**Virginia Apgar**

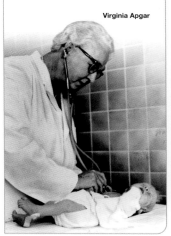

**THE MEDICAL USE OF LASERS**
Laser surgery works when a beam of light, the laser,
is concentrated on a target area. It can be used to seal
a blood vessel, correct vision, or destroy harmful cells.
One German inventor has filed more than 100 patents
relating to improving laser surgery. Here, lasers are
used to create reference lines for a scanner.

**Laser beams are used for a huge range of tasks, from cutting diamonds to use in**

# surgery

# Engineering marvels

Engineering covers the design and building of the machines and structures that surround us, and makes our lives easier. There have been a number of key inventions in the field of engineering, especially in the last 200 years, but the use of simple machines dates back much further. Here, the Falkirk Wheel links two Scottish canals by lifting and lowering boats.

**SCREWDRIVER**
The screwdriver is a simple but incredibly useful tool. We know that screwdrivers were used in Europe in the 1400s.

# How machines work

Can you think of a simple machine? One common example is a hammer, which makes the task of hitting a nail into wood much easier. The hammer is an example of a lever, one of a number of simple machines that are at the heart of many more complicated inventions.

### Wheel and axle

An axle passes through the centre of a wheel and together they work as a rotating machine, making it easier to move an object. A roundabout is an example of a wheel and axle put to use in playgrounds the world over.

Axle

### Lever

A lever works by either magnifying or reducing a force. Drinks cans use a simple lever to make them easy to open.

### Gears

These cogs show how gears work. Gears are toothed wheels that work together to increase speed or force.

### Inclined plane

Slopes, known as inclined planes, make it easier to push or pull an object, rather than lifting it.

### Screw

Screws convert the force that is turning them, by means of a ridged shaft, to drive them into a material such as wood.

### Pulley

A pulley consists of a length of rope wrapped around a wheel. It is used to lift.

### Wedge

### Wedge

Wedges increase force. An axe has a wedge-shaped head that can be used to split wood.

## COMPLEX MACHINES

The success of simple machines led to the invention of increasingly complicated ones that combined two or more simple machines. A bicycle contains several simple machines.

Wheel

Levers

Gears

## FOCUS ON...
## ENERGY

People have developed various machines for collecting the energy required to drive other machinery.

▲ Wind turbines use the wind's power to make electricity.

▲ Solar panels convert sunlight to electricity.

▲ Nuclear power plants make electricity by splitting atoms in a reactor.

# Machines

Inventions in the field of machinery have completely transformed the way we live, speeding up tasks that previously took days to a matter of hours, and making the previously impossible possible.

### Plough

A plough uses a ploughshare to turn over the soil, readying it for seeds. Early ploughs were pulled or pushed by people, but by 4000 BCE farmers were using oxen. Later still, wheels were added for use over heavier soils.

Wooden frame

Metal ploughshare

| | |
|---|---|
| **INVENTED BY** | Unknown |
| **WHEN** | 6000 BCE |
| **WHERE** | Mesopotamia (modern-day Iraq) |

## Windmill

In the first century CE a windwheel was used to pump air to play music on an organ. It was invented by Greek engineer Hero of Alexandria, but it was very different from later windmills which were used for pumping and for milling grain. They emerged in Persia.

**INVENTED BY** Unknown

**WHEN** c.850 CE

**WHERE** Persia

— Rotating sails

## Crane

There's a limit to the amount a person can lift. As the demand for larger buildings grew, the invention of cranes to lift heavy blocks of stone became necessary.

**INVENTED BY** Unknown

**WHEN** 520 BCE

**WHERE** Greece

## Canal lock

A lock in a canal is a device for raising or lowering a boat so that an artificial canal can cross hills. Some of the world's first canals were built in China more than 1,200 years ago.

**INVENTED BY** Chhiao (or Qiao) Wei-Yo

**WHEN** 983 CE

**WHERE** China

## Seed drill

A seed drill
sows seeds in
rows. Until the
invention of the seed drill,
farmers sowed seeds by
scattering them, creating a lot of
waste. Jethro Tull invented an
automatic seed drill in the eighteenth
century. Simple seed drills had been
used by the Babylonians, but Tull's seed
drill sowed three rows of seeds at once.

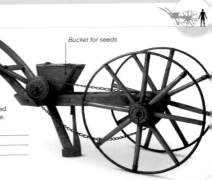

*Bucket for seeds*

**INVENTED BY** Jethro Tull

**WHEN** 1701

**WHERE** England

## Spinning jenny

A spinning wheel (thought to have been
invented in the eleventh century) spins one
thread from wool at a time. The spinning
jenny speeded up the process because it could spin
several threads at once. When it was invented,
people feared it would
mean the loss of
a lot of jobs.

**INVENTED BY**
James
Hargreaves

**WHEN**
1764

**WHERE**
England

## Cotton gin

The cotton gin was built to separate
cotton fibres from the unwanted seeds.
It consisted of a revolving, hooked cylinder.
The hooks caught the seeds
and forced
them through
a comb,
removing
the fibres.

**INVENTED BY**
Eli Whitney

**WHEN** 1793

**WHERE** USA

# Steam engine

An English engineer named Thomas Newcomen built the world's first steam-powered engine. It was an inefficient machine, but it remained the best engine for the next 50 years. It was used to pump water out of coal and tin mines – flooding was a huge problem.

| | |
|---|---|
| **INVENTED BY** | Thomas Newcomen |
| **WHEN** | 1710 |
| **WHERE** | England |

**Model of one of Newcomen's engines**

Steam power, in the form of steam turbines, is still in use today in almost every power station.

*Water was heated in this boiler*

## Tunnel boring machine (TBM)

The need to tunnel through hills and mountains when building roads has long been a problem. The first attempt at a machine to do the job came in the 1840s, with the "Mountain Slicer". However, it was an inefficient machine.

**INVENTED BY** Henri-Joseh Maus

**WHEN** 1846

**WHERE** France and Italy

This TBM, built in the late 1980s, was used to dig part of the Channel Tunnel that links England with France.

## Oil well

Drilling for oil has seen enormous oil fields on land and oil rigs at sea. For hundreds of years, people had collected oil as it oozed out of a soft rock called shale. Somebody then realized that the process may be faster if they dug down. The first oil well was dug by Edwin Drake on land owned by George Bissell.

**INVENTED BY** Edwin Drake and George Bissell

**WHEN** 1859

**WHERE** USA

## Tractor (petrol-powered)

The tractors we see today are an invention that has developed over many years. Early tractors were powered by steam, but they had limited success. Petrol-powered tractors were far lighter and more powerful.

**INVENTED BY** Herbert Akroyd Stuart

**WHEN** 1901

**WHERE** England

Tractor (1917)

## Dragline

A dragline is used to excavate a large site, often for mining. The first dragline was used to help dig out a channel for the Chicago Canal, USA, when enormous amounts of earth had to be shifted. The dragline shown below operates at a coal mine in Australia.

**INVENTED BY** John W Page

**WHEN** 1904

**WHERE** USA

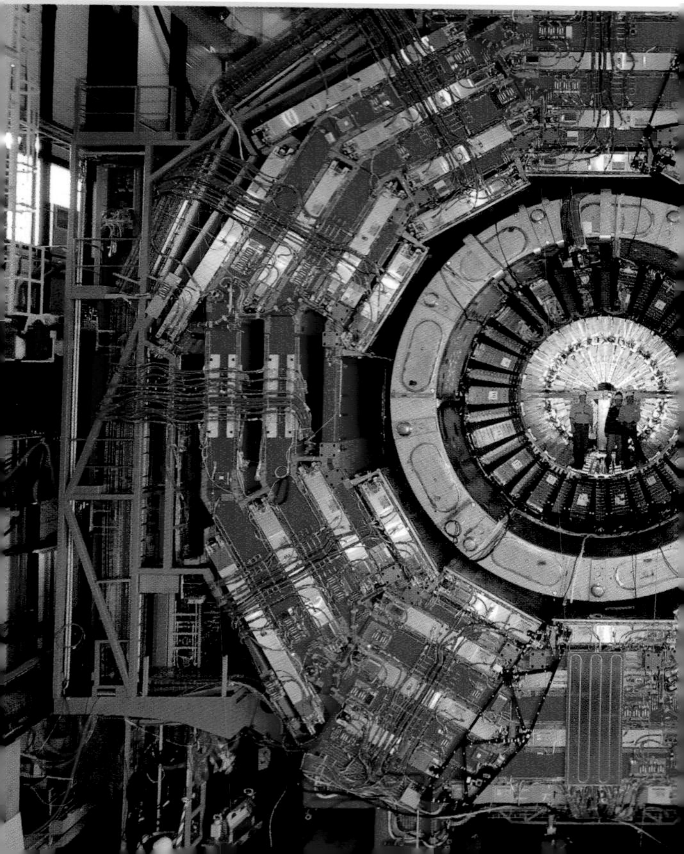

# The Large Hadron Collider is the world's largest machine. It stretches for

# 27 km

## (17 miles).

**LARGE HADRON COLLIDER (LHC)**

Everything you see is made up of atoms (which you cannot see). In turn, atoms are made of particles. The LHC has been built so that scientists can learn more about particles, and so help them know more about the Universe – particularly how it began and what it is made of.

## Earthquake detector (seismoscope)

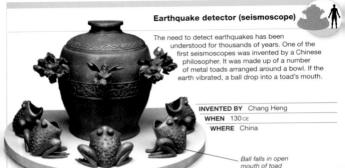

The need to detect earthquakes has been understood for thousands of years. One of the first seismoscopes was invented by a Chinese philosopher. It was made up of a number of metal toads arranged around a bowl. If the earth vibrated, a ball drop into a toad's mouth.

**INVENTED BY**  Chang Heng

**WHEN**  130 CE

**WHERE**  China

*Ball falls in open mouth of toad*

## Seismographs

A seismograph records ground vibrations as a zigzag line. It is an important tool in helping to predict earthquakes, but is also used for oil exploration. Today's machines date back to an invention by John Milne in 1880, but there was an earlier seismograph.

**INVENTED BY**  Felippo Cecchi

**WHEN**  1875

**WHERE**  Italy

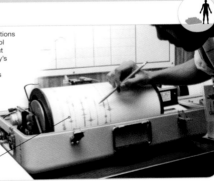

*Lines on paper record ground vibrations*

## Smoke detector

Many lives have been saved thanks to this invention. It had a long history of development before appearing in a form suitable for people's homes. The first alarm was based on sensing a room's temperature rather than smoke.

| | |
|---|---|
| **INVENTED BY** | George Andrew Darby |
| **WHEN** | 1902 |
| **WHERE** | England |

## Flight recorder

An aeroplane crash is a rare event, but if there is a crash, a flight recorder helps investigators understand what has happened as it records everything that goes on in the cockpit.

| | |
|---|---|
| **INVENTED BY** | Dr David Warren |
| **WHEN** | 1958 |
| **WHERE** | Australia |

## Radar

People had already discovered that radio waves bounced off metal objects. The British government wanted to see if they could be used as a weapon to destroy aeroplanes in wartime. Looking into this, a Scottish engineer managed to use radio waves to detect aircraft.

| | |
|---|---|
| **INVENTED BY** | Robert Watson-Watt |
| **WHEN** | 1935 |
| **WHERE** | England |

# Telescopes

There is evidence that simple lenses were used thousands of years ago. However, the development of lenses – to improve vision or build telescopes, for example, was a slow process. Even more of an engineering marvel is the fact that we now have a number of telescopes in space.

## Telescope

The discovery that putting two lenses together could enlarge distant objects was key to the invention of the telescope. Surprisingly, the first telescope didn't appear until the early 1600s. It was invented by a Dutch spectacle maker and put to good use by Italian scientist Galileo Galilei.

**INVENTED BY**
Hans Lippershey
**WHEN** 1608
**WHERE**
The Netherlands

Replica of telescope designed by Galileo (1610)

## Lens

In the eighth century BCE, the Mesopotamians understood that curved pieces of glass (or lenses) refract light. One of the oldest lenses ever found is known as the Nimrud or Layard lens. The name "lens" comes from the Latin word for lentil – because lenses are lentil-shaped.

**INVENTED BY** Unknown
**WHEN** 700 BCE
**WHERE** Mesopotamia (modern-day Iraq)

## Non-reflecting glass

The invention of non-reflecting glass was a major step forwards for the use of glass, especially that used to make lenses. This "invisible" glass was much better than previous types for things such as eyewear, telescopes, and camera lenses.

**INVENTED BY**
Katharine Blodgett, Irving Langmuir
**WHEN** 1938
**WHERE** USA

Katharine Blodgett

## Space telescope

The idea of a space telescope was first suggested by German rocket scientist Hermann Oberth in 1923, who realized that it would have a clearer view of the Universe than a land-based telescope. He was way ahead of the available technology. The first space-based optical telescope was the Hubble Space Telescope, which is still operating.

**INVENTED BY** Lyman Spitzer and NASA

**WHEN** 1990

**WHERE** USA

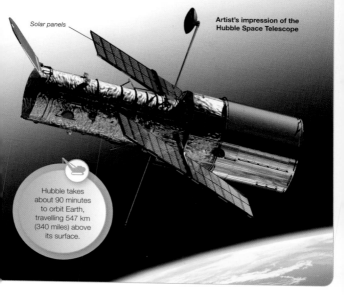

Solar panels

**Artist's impression of the Hubble Space Telescope**

Hubble takes about 90 minutes to orbit Earth, travelling 547 km (340 miles) above its surface.

## FOCUS ON...
## POWER

We need power to make many of the inventions around us work. Much of this power is made in massive power plants.

▲ Generators create electricity at power plants, using coal, gas, nuclear power, or water.

▲ Transformers at power plants increase electrical voltage so that power can be transmitted at lower cost.

▲ Power lines carry the electricity needed for homes, schools, and offices from a power plant.

# Infrastructure

Look around you. The roads and bridges, tunnels and skyscrapers that you see were all built by people. They are part of the basic features, or infrastructure, a country needs to work smoothly. They all have a history as to their invention.

### Roads

Glance outside your window and the chances are you'll see a road. We depend on roads to move around easily but they weren't always so extensive. The first roads appeared some 5,500 years ago in Persia. One of the longest early roads stretched for 2,857 km (1,785 miles), from the Persian Gulf to the Aegean Sea.

| | |
|---|---|
| **INVENTED BY** | Unknown |
| **WHEN** | c.3500 BCE |
| **WHERE** | Persia |

## Suspension bridge

It's hard to imagine life without bridges. Some of the earliest suspension bridges (which hang from cables) were designed by Thangtong Gyalpo in the 1400s. Incredibly, some (like this one in Bhutan) are still used today.

**INVENTED BY** Thangtong Gyalpo

**WHEN** c.1430

**WHERE** Tibet and Bhutan

## Skyscraper

Some people work in a skyscraper, a tall building with a steel structure. The first skyscraper was designed by an American engineer, William Jenney, and completed in 1885. It was 10 storeys high. So many inventions contributed to the skyscraper that no one inventor can be credited.

**INVENTED BY** Unknown

**WHEN** 1880s

**WHERE** USA

**Petronas Towers, Malaysia**

## Dam

A dam is a structure purpose-built to hold back water and, in some cases, provide electricity. One of the earliest known dams (the Jawa Dam) was built in Jordan as a water storage system.

**INVENTED BY** Unknown

**WHEN** c.3000 BCE

**WHERE** Mesopotamia (modern-day Iraq)

# Arms and ammunition

Warfare dates back to prehistory, but many weapons known for their use in war were developed from tools and first used by early people for hunting. The spear and the bow and arrow are perfect examples of this.

## Spear

*Wooden shaft*

*Sinew or leather binding*

There is evidence that our early ancestors were throwing spears in South Africa some 500,000 yeas ago. Archaeologists discovered a number of stone points at one site that they believe were the tips of what would have been spears.

## Bow and arrow

We know that bows and arrows were used for hunting some 30,000 years ago. Although none have survived from this time, they are shown in cave paintings. The first arrows would have been made of wood, but in around 18,000 BCE, people learned how to carve flint arrowheads and attach these to a shaft.

| INVENTED BY | Unknown |
| WHEN | 30,000 years ago |
| WHERE | Africa |

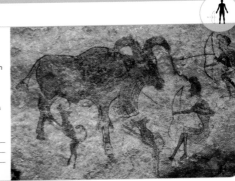

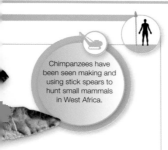

Chimpanzees have been seen making and using stick spears to hunt small mammals in West Africa.

**INVENTED BY** Unknown
**WHEN** 500,000 years ago
**WHERE** Africa

## Sword

Metal swords developed in the Bronze Age when it became possible to make longer weapons than a dagger. However, the problem with bronze is that a longer sword will bend, so stronger swords (used for fighting) were only developed with the later use of steel. Shown here is a fifteenth-century sword.

*Bronze blade*

*Gold pommel*

**INVENTED BY** Unknown
**WHEN** 3300 BCE
**WHERE** Unknown

## Guns

The first guns didn't look like the guns of today. They are known as Chinese fire lances, and were basically a tube made from bamboo or metal. They were filled with gunpowder and shrapnel and fired at a target. The hand cannon also developed from this invention.

**Hand cannon**

**INVENTED BY** Chinese
**WHEN** 900 CE
**WHERE** China

## Dynamite

Although dynamite has been used in war, it was actually invented by Alfred Nobel, the founder of the Nobel Peace Prize. It was developed from gunpowder (long after the discovery of gunpowder) as a more stable explosive. It has been used in construction, in mining, and for tunnelling.

**INVENTED BY** Alfred Nobel
**WHEN** 1867
**WHERE** Sweden

# Tools

The first tools were simply stones that could be used to smash open bones and hack away at meat. In time, people began to chip away at the edges of these stones, to shape them and make a sharp cutting edge. Later, they discovered metal.

## FOCUS ON... KNAPPING

Knapping is a method of chipping away at a stone to make it into a tool. This is how early humans made tools.

▲ First, a hammerstone was used to chip away large flakes of stone.

▲ Next, the hammerstone was used to grind the stone to shape it.

▲ Finally, bones or antlers were used to create a thin, sharp edge.

### Hand axe

The first tools were grasped in the hand and used to grind, chop, and cut. Flint was the preferred material for making tools in the Old Stone Age (the Paleolithic period) as it was readily available and easy to shape. The Old Stone Age lasted from the first use of stone tools until the end of the last ice age.

| | |
|---|---|
| **INVENTED BY** | Unknown |
| **WHEN** | c.1.8 million years ago |
| **WHERE** | Kenya |

*Sharp edge acted like a knife's blade.*

## Drill

The earliest drills used a wooden bow that was pushed back and forth to spin a pointed wooden stick (the bit) and drill holes for thousands of years.

**INVENTED BY** Unknown
**WHEN** c.35000 BCE
**WHERE** Unknown

## Chisel

A chisel has a sharpened blade at the end, not along the side (like a knife). Chisels are used for carving objects from wood or soft stone. Many sculptures have been created thanks to the invention of the chisel.

**INVENTED BY** Unknown
**WHEN** c.7000 BCE
**WHERE** Unknown

## Sickle

The sickle was one of the first tools invented to help harvest crops. Early sickles were made of a stone called flint and had short, straight blades. Sickles are still used, but they have a curved blade.

**INVENTED BY** Unknown
**WHEN** c.7000 BCE
**WHERE** Unknown

**Modern sickle with curved metal blade**

## Power drill

The invention of the electric motor led to the invention of all sorts of tools, some, like the power drill, incredibly useful in the home. The first power drill wasn't portable, unlike the battery-powered drills used today.

**Modern portable drill**

**INVENTED BY** Arthur James Arnot (Scottish born) and William Blanch Brain
**WHEN** 1889
**WHERE** Australia

# It is estimated that
# 15 billion
# aerosol cans
## are produced worldwide each year

**AEROSOLS**
An aerosol can works because pressurized gas forces a liquid from the container as a spray. The cans we use date to an invention by Norwegian chemical engineer Erik Rotheim in 1926. The idea of adding paint to an aerosol can was first tried by American businessman Edward Seymour in 1949, who credited his wife Bonnie with the idea.

# Nanotechnology

This is the science of creating materials and simple machines that are too small to see, even with the help of a normal microscope. Nanotechnology is now used in all sorts of everyday products, from sunscreens to textiles.

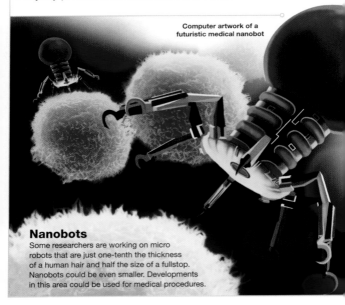

Computer artwork of a futuristic medical nanobot

## Nanobots

Some researchers are working on micro robots that are just one-tenth the thickness of a human hair and half the size of a fullstop. Nanobots could be even smaller. Developments in this area could be used for medical procedures.

## Clothes

Nanotechnology is increasingly being used in clothing. Particles called "nanowhiskers" prevent stains or water from sticking to fabric so stain-resistant and waterproof clothing can be made. Odour-resistant socks also contain nanoparticles.

**Magnified image of a fabric with a waterproof coating**

## Sunscreens

Many sunscreens used to leave white marks on the skin. Nanoparticles of metal oxides now used in some sunscreens offer protection – and also avoid the white streaks.

## STILL SMALL

Miniature lens

Although too large to count as nanotechnology, it is now possible for a patient to swallow a camera the size of a large tablet, providing doctors with a view of their insides. The capsule contains a camera, radio transmitter, battery, and light source.

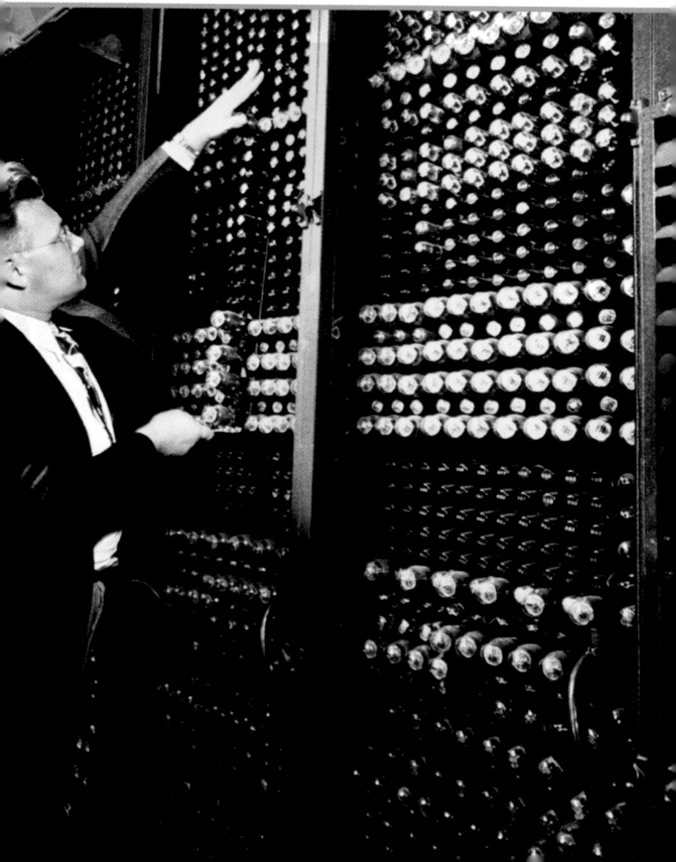

# Information technology

Humans have been storing, retrieving, and sharing information since the Sumerians in Mesopotamia developed writing in about 3000 BCE. Today, we have computers and data storage devices such as USB flash drives and DVDs. One of the first general-purpose electronic computers was called the Electronic Numerical Integrator and Computer, or ENIAC (left). It filled a room!

**FIRST MOUSE**
The American engineer Douglas Engelbart invented the computer mouse in 1963. It was named a mouse because its cord looked like a tail.

# Communication

We now have a huge variety of choices for communication. However, the realization that there could be more ways of communicating than handwritten messages and direct conversation came relatively recently. Inventions in this area really only took off in the last 150 years or so.

## A quick hello

If you have a friend or family member who lives far away, you can choose from a variety of ways to get in touch. Billions of emails are sent every day, but there are faster ways to chat, from texting to video calling (VC) to instant messaging (IM).

Facebook

Instagram

Twitter

## Social media

Various platforms allow people to "talk" via their phones and computers. Online forums allow people to exchange ideas, photo sharing sites allow the display of photographs, and social networking sites allow users to create a public profile and share connections.

Messaging app in use

Illustration of a weather satellite in orbit

## The power of satellites

Hundreds of satellites orbit Earth, enabling information to be sent from one side of the world to the other in a matter of seconds. It's an important part of today's communication system. For example, we receive weather forecasts thanks to special satellites.

## The wonder of fibre optics

In the early days of the telephone, cables contained paper-insulated wires enclosed in a metal casing. Fibre-optic technology has changed our communications dramatically, with a single fibre capable of carrying thousands of telephone circuits.

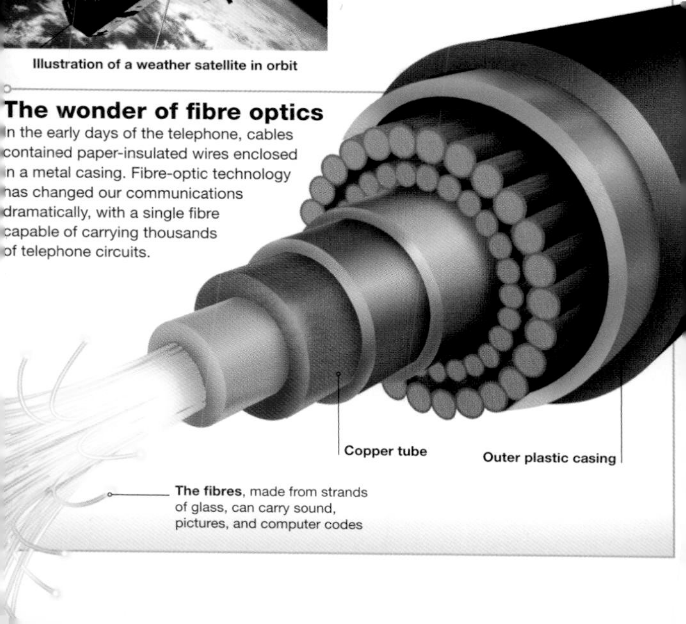

Copper tube

Outer plastic casing

The fibres, made from strands of glass, can carry sound, pictures, and computer codes

# Paper and printing

Six hundred years ago, most books were copied by hand. It was a lengthy process and one that held up the spread of information. It's hard to imagine such a world – a world without today's easy access to the written word. The invention of the printing press changed the way books were made for ever.

**Papyrus**

This paper-like material is made from the papyrus plant. The ancient Egyptians used it to write on, but it was fragile and tended to crack. This papyrus fragment depicts oxen and is dated from around 1450 BCE.

**INVENTED BY** Unknown

**WHEN** c.3000 BCE

**WHERE** Egypt and Southern Sudan

## Paper

The oldest fragments of paper
we have date from around
50 BCE. Paper was invented
in China and news of its
usefulness spread gradually.
Paper mills did not begin
to appear in Europe,
for example, until
the 1100s.

**INVENTED BY** Unknown
**WHEN** c.50 BCE
**WHERE** China

## Book

Early books were
all hand-written
and had no
pages – they
were written on
rolls of papyrus or
scratched onto
wood or clay
tablets. As books became longer, binding
separate pages along one edge to form a codex
made them easier to handle. They became
standard in the 300s.

**INVENTED BY** Unknown
**WHEN** c.350 CE
**WHERE** Unknown

## Movable type and the printing press

Movable type first appeared in China in the
eleventh century, invented by Bi Sheng. However,
they didn't suit Chinese writing, which uses
hundreds of characters, so little use was made
of it. In fifteenth-century Germany, a jeweller
called Johannes Gutenberg invented a speedier
method of typecasting using metal moulds
and a printing press (adapted from
previous olive and wine presses).

**INVENTED BY** Johannes Gutenberg
**WHEN** 1455
**WHERE** Germany

*Movable type is
single letter on
individual blocks*

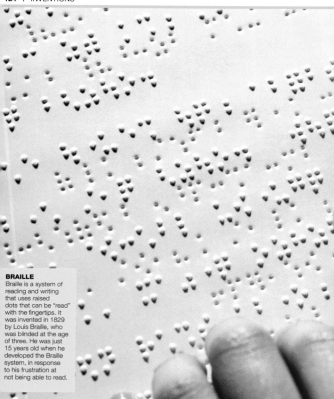

**BRAILLE**
Braille is a system of reading and writing that uses raised dots that can be "read" with the fingertips. It was invented in 1829 by Louis Braille, who was blinded at the age of three. He was just 15 years old when he developed the Braille system, in response to his frustration at not being able to read.

Braille is based on
# six dots in a cell.
### There are 63 possible combinations of these dots to provide different letters.

# Telephones

For centuries, people have tried to send signals over long distances using bonfires and flashing mirrors. In 1876, Alexander Graham Bell invented the telephone, enabling speech to be sent along wires for the first time.

## FOCUS ON...
## CODES

Communication at a distance originally involved the use of codes that had to be deciphered.

▲ The Semaphore system uses two flags held in different positions to signal letters and numbers.

```
A  • –
B  – • • •
0  – – – – –
1  • – – – –
2  • • – – –
```

▲ In Morse code, text information is relayed as a series of pulses of different lengths.

▲ A telegram is a written message conveyed using an electric device and a huge web of wires.

### Telephone

On 10 March 1876, Scottish inventor Alexander Graham Bell conveyed the first successful message through a telephone to his assistant, Thomas Watson – "Mr Watson... come here... I want to see you".

| | |
|---|---|
| **INVENTED BY** | Alexander Graham Bell |
| **WHEN** | 1876 |
| **WHERE** | USA |

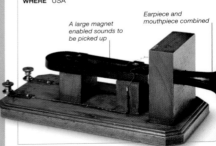

A large magnet enabled sounds to be picked up

Earpiece and mouthpiece combined

## Automatic telephone exchange

As telephones became popular in the home, one problem became apparent. The calls had to be put through by operators, who could listen in to calls or even misdirect them (the inventor believed this had happened to him, affecting his business). The invention of the automatic telephone exchange meant telephone operators were no longer needed.

**INVENTED BY** Almon Strowger

**WHEN** 1889

**WHERE** USA

A manual telephone exchange (1945)

## Hand-held mobile phone

The first hand-held mobile phone call was made in New York City in 1973 from a phone the size of a brick – it weighed 2 kg (4.4 lb) and was 23 cm (9 in) long.

**INVENTED BY** Martin Cooper (working at Motorola)

**WHEN** 1975

**WHERE** USA

Martin Cooper

## Smartphone

The smartphone is a pocket computer that can also be used to make phone calls, shoot video, play music, and many more functions. Most smartphones have a touch screen – a visual display that allows users to access features on the phone by touching it.

**INVENTED BY** IBM

**WHEN** 1993

**WHERE** USA

iPhone, a smartphone built by Apple

# Still and moving pictures

A lot of information is passed around the world and into our homes in picture form – either via still images or films. Technology in this area moves fast – the first television, for example, was soon superceded by a better invention.

### Camera obscura

The cameras we use today began life as a "camera obscura", which means "a dark room". The dark room had a tiny hole in one wall that let light through. On the wall opposite the hole, a fuzzy image appeared, though upside down. This can occur naturally, but in 1558 an Italian physicist put a lens in the hole, which focused the light to produce a sharper image.

**INVENTED BY**
Giambattista della Porta

**WHEN** 1558

**WHERE** Italy

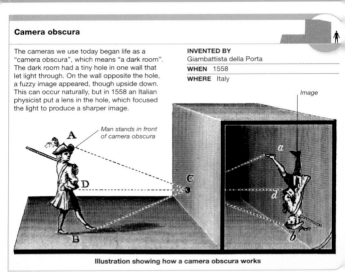

Man stands in front of camera obscura

Image

Illustration showing how a camera obscura works

## Daguerreotype photographic process

Images seen in the camera obscura were often copied by artists, but one man, Louis Daguerre, wanted to find an easier way to keep the image. He discovered a method of producing the image on a silver-plated copper sheet. Daguerre took this picture in Paris in 1838.

**INVENTED BY** Louis Jacques Mandé Daguerre

**WHEN** 1835

**WHERE** France

## Roll film

The first cameras used plates to record images, but the invention of a camera with film on a reel meant that the camera could be smaller, making it more portable.

**INVENTED BY** George Eastman

**WHEN** 1888

**WHERE** USA

*Film is placed into a camera*

## Polaroid camera

The Polaroid camera was an exciting invention as it produced instant results – the photograph appeared in about 60 seconds. Polaroid produced one million of these cameras between 1948 and 1956.

**INVENTED BY** Edwin H Land

**WHEN** 1948

**WHERE** USA

*The picture is produced from the camera*

## Electronic television

John Logie Baird had invented a mechanical television (he called it a "televisor") in the 1920s, but the pictures were fuzzy and the invention of the electronic television proved the way forwards. Electronic televisions use a cathode-ray tube (a device for showing images on a screen).

**INVENTED BY**
Vladimir Zworykin,
Isaac Shoenberg

**WHEN** 1936

**WHERE** USA
and England

John Logie Baird's first television was made from tea chests, biscuit tins, and a darning needle.

**1960s television**

## LCD TV

Televisions today use a flat liquid-crystal display (LCD), instead of a cathode ray tube, and digital technology. A lot of people worked on liquid-crystal technology, but the real breakthrough came when American inventor James Fergason discovered a type of liquid crystal that was far better than anything developed before.

**INVENTED BY** Martin Schadt, Wolfgang Heinrich, James Fergason

**WHEN** 1971

**WHERE** Switzerland and USA

## Digital camera

Today most smartphones contain a digital camera. The first electronic camera dates back to 1975, but it was very different from those we use today. It weighed 3.6 kg (8 lbs) and it took 23 seconds to record each image (in black and white).

**INVENTED BY** Steven Sasson
**WHEN** 1975
**WHERE** USA

Modern digital camera

## Film developing methods

Before digital photography took over, film development could be tricky. In 1978, a scientist called Barbara Askins invented a method of developing film that helped to show more detail in photographs. Though no longer used, at the time it was important as it revealed previously invisible parts of a photograph or a negative. It enabled scientists to see more in space photographs as well as helping in the development of X-rays.

**INVENTED BY** Barbara Askins
**WHEN** 1978
**WHERE** USA

# The coming of computers

Charles Babbage attempted to design a "computer" to carry out difficult calculations as early as the 1830s. However, little progress was made until the 1940s.

FOCUS ON...
## STORAGE
Today, much computer data is stored on "clouds". It wasn't always this way.

## Vacuum tubes (valves)

These bulky tubes were electrical components that acted as switches (a switch makes or breaks an electrical circuit) or amplify electrical signals (making them stronger). An impressive 17,468 vacuum tubes were used in the computer ENIAC, built in 1946 (radios of the time used just five!). The vacuum tube looked like a light bulb. It was unreliable, tending to overheat.

Vacuum tube

| | |
|---|---|
| **INVENTED BY** | Lee De Forest |
| **WHEN** | 1906 |
| **WHERE** | USA |

## Colossus

This was the first general-purpose programmable electronic computer. It was developed three years before ENIAC (see p.118), but its existence was kept a secret until recently. It was used for wartime code-breaking. A replica is now on display in a museum at Bletchley Park, England, where Colossus was built.

| | |
|---|---|
| **INVENTED BY** | Tommy Flowers |
| **WHEN** | 1943 |
| **WHERE** | England |

◀ Holes punched in paper tape was a way of storing data for computers in the 1950s and 1960s.

▶ Floppy storage disks first appeared in 1971. The disk was protected by a hard case.

▲ USB flash drives first appeared in the late 1990s. These can store larger amounts of data than floppies.

## Transistor

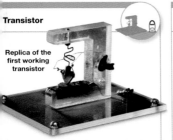

Replica of the first working transistor

A transistor controls electric current, doing the same job as a valve. However, it is smaller and its invention therefore meant the technology using it could be smaller. Designs got smaller and smaller, thanks to the later invention of the microchip. Today, hundreds of millions of transistors can fit on a single computer chip.

**INVENTED BY** John Bardeen, Walter Brattain, William Shockley

**WHEN** 1947

**WHERE** USA

## Microchip

The electronic parts of early computers were connected by hand, limiting how small these parts could be. A microchip combines the components on a circuit made of a semi-conducting material. Its invention meant that many components could be laid on just one wafer of silicon.

**INVENTED BY** Jack Kilby and Robert Noyce

**WHEN** 1958

**WHERE** USA

In 1997 ENIAC was recreated on just one silicon chip!

## Personal computer (PC)

PCs are now common – they are small enough to be easily transportable, inexpensive, and simple to use. There's been a lot of debate about which was the first such computer, but one of the first, the Apple, is still going strong (though it looks very different from the first model).

**Early Apple computer in wood case**

| INVENTED BY | Steve Jobs and Stephen Wozniak |
| --- | --- |
| WHEN | 1977 |
| WHERE | USA |

## Microprocessor

A microprocessor controls a computer's functions, from running the operating system to recognizing which keys are pressed. Despite this, microprocessors are tiny. Microprocessors make personal computers and smart appliances (such as washing machines) possible. The first one was the Intel 4004.

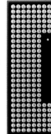

| INVENTED BY | Ted Hoff |
| --- | --- |
| WHEN | 1971 |
| WHERE | USA |

## Supercomputer

Governments, universities, and big businesses depend on supercomputers to handle computing tasks. They can perform billions of tasks each second. Electrical engineer Seymour Cray worked on the world's first supercomputer, shown here, Cray-1.

| INVENTED BY | Seymour Cray |
| --- | --- |
| WHEN | 1976 |
| WHERE | USA |

## 3-D printers

The idea of a printer that can generate 3-D objects dates back some 30 years. The first such printer was very different from those in use today, but it started the development. Today's 3-D printers build objects by using layers of plastic.

*Objects are built with thin layers of plastic*

| INVENTED BY | Chuck Hull |
| --- | --- |
| WHEN | 1984 |
| WHERE | USA |

THE COMING OF COMPUTERS **| 135**

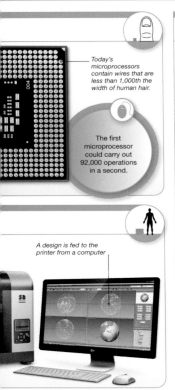

*Today's microprocessors contain wires that are less than 1,000th the width of human hair.*

004

The first microprocessor could carry out 92,000 operations in a second.

*A design is fed to the printer from a computer*

## Tablet

These computers lack a physical keyboard but provide instant online access and are easily portable. The first touch-screen tablet appeared in 2000, launched by Bill Gates at Microsoft, but it wasn't a huge success. The first truly successful tablet was the iPad, launched in 2010.

| | |
|---|---|
| **INVENTED BY** | Microsoft |
| **WHEN** | 2000 |
| **WHERE** | USA |

**Apple iPad**

## Internet

The realization that computers could be linked to share information led to the development of the Internet we know today. The Internet links millions of individual computers, tablets, and phones around the world, so they can exchange information. The idea began with a need to link research computers and was first developed under the name ARPAnet. This developed into the Internet in 1983.

**INVENTED BY** J C R Licklider and Larry Roberts
**WHEN** 1983
**WHERE** USA and England

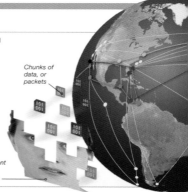

*Chunks of data, or packets*

*Image to be sent is broken into chunks of data*

## World Wide Web (WWW)

The web is the collection of pages of data (web pages), including music files, digital photographs, and films, that can be accessed over the Internet. It is called a web because all these things are linked – web pages are connected by hypertext links.

**INVENTED BY** Tim Berners-Lee
**WHEN** 1989
**WHERE** Switzerland

**Tim Berners-Lee**

## Browser

A browser is a program on a computer that is used to access the Internet. The first widely used web browser was developed by a 21-year-old student. It was called Mosaic. Today, the most popular browser is Google Chrome.

**Google Chrome**

**Safari**

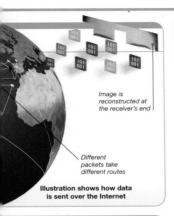

*Image is reconstructed at the receiver's end*

*Different packets take different routes*

**Illustration shows how data is sent over the Internet**

## Wi-Fi technology

Wi-Fi hotspots allow us to go online in many places, from homes and schools to airports. Connecting to the Internet remotely (without wires) was proving tricky, until an Australian research agency invented a chip that made Wi-Fi reliable.

| | |
|---|---|
| **INVENTED BY** | Many inventors |
| **WHEN** | 1997 |
| **WHERE** | USA and Australia |

| | |
|---|---|
| **INVENTED BY** | Marc Andreessen and Eric Bina |
| **WHEN** | 1993 |
| **WHERE** | USA |

**Internet Explorer**     **Firefox**

## Search engine

Search engines help web users to find information by searching for a word or phrase. The first successful full-text search engine, Lycos, was launched in 1994. Today's most widely used search engine is Google (invented in 1998).

| | |
|---|---|
| **INVENTED BY** | Michael Loren Maudlin |
| **WHEN** | 1994 |
| **WHERE** | USA |

www.dk.com

**SEARCH**

**SATELLITES**
A huge number of artificial satellites have been sent into space to orbit Earth. They take pictures, conduct experiments, and relay signals. We depend on them for all sorts of information and for communication. However, this also means there is a lot of space debris, shown by this computer-generated image.